CLIVEDEN

The Place and The People

'When one lives in Paradise, how hard it must be to ascend
in heart and mind to Heaven!'

The Diary of Lady Frederick Cavendish
on Cliveden, June 1863

'The poetry of History lies in the quasi-miraculous fact that
once on this earth, once on this familiar spot of ground,
walked other men and women, as actual as we are today,
thinking their own thoughts, ravaged by their own passions,
but now all gone, one generation vanishing after another,
gone as utterly as we ourselves will shortly be gone, like a
ghost at cockcrow.'

G. M. Trevelyan

CLIVEDEN

The Place and The People

JAMES CRATHORNE

COLLINS & BROWN

First published in Great Britain in 1995 by
Collins & Brown Limited
London House
Great Eastern Wharf
Parkgate Road
London SW11 4NQ

1 3 5 7 9 8 6 4 2

British Library Cataloguing-in-Publication Data:
A catalogue record for this book is available from
the British Library

ISBN 1 85585 223 3

Designed by Toucan Books Limited, London

Reproduction by CH Colourscan, Malaysia

Printed and bound in Italy by New Interlitho SpA

ENDPAPERS: Cliefden House, Buckinghamshire,
an engraving from a drawing by Corbould,
published in 1742.

PAGE i: *Alexander Monro's design for a sculptural relief on the*
south façade of Cliveden.

PAGE iii: Spring, *one of the Four Seasons designed by*
Alexander Monro.

Contents

Acknowledgements

I WOULD LIKE TO THANK Her Majesty The Queen for her gracious permission to quote from the letters and diaries of Queen Victoria; also Her Royal Highness Princess Margaret for her memory of Nancy Astor.

Grateful thanks are due to William Astor (the present Viscount Astor), who has written the Foreword and checked the manuscript, and given permission for the use of numerous illustrations. He has also been involved with the creation of the hotel at Cliveden. Thanks are due, too, to David Astor (Nancy Astor's son), who has been through the manuscript in detail and made various suggestions. Bronwen, Viscountess Astor provided two illustrations; Lord Astor of Hever showed me round Hever Castle, Kent; Alice Winn (Nancy Astor's niece) and her daughter Elizabeth Winn made helpful comments on the text.

Many thanks go to Gervase Jackson-Stops, Architectural Adviser to the National Trust, who has published indispensable articles on Cliveden; he not only allowed me access to all his research papers but went through my manuscript making corrections and suggestions. National Trust officers at the Thames and Chilterns Regional Office who have helped are Christopher Wall, Anthea Palmer and Jonathan Marsden who compiled the most recent National Trust Cliveden guide and was particularly helpful with the Sutherland chapter. Thanks also to Don Kennedy and Philip Cotton of the National Trust at Cliveden. The National Trust's architect for Cliveden, Julian Harrap, and Cliveden Hotel's architect, William Bertram, spoke to me at length about the restoration of the building.

Others who have helped include the following: the Earl of Jersey, who arranged for me to see the Duke of Buckingham's Commonplace Book and Joan Coburn, head archivist, G.L.C. Record Office, who arranged the photography; Tony Packe, of Burnham, who has had a lifelong interest in the history of Cliveden and Taplow; Dr Graham Haslam, former archivist, and Elisabeth Stuart, present archivist, to the Duchy of Cornwall, which is in possession of the account books of Frederick, Prince of Wales; Michael Bott of Reading University Library, where there is a large archive of Astor material; Geoffrey Tyack, Director of Stanford University in England, who did much research into life at Cliveden between the wars and who told me about Stanford University's time at Cliveden, later scrutinizing and adding to the text; Lord Bruntisfield and his brother Robin Warrender, who made available Sir George Warrender's Letter Books and permitted the use of the portrait of Sir George as an illustration; Mrs Sarah Markham, who gave permission to quote from her edition of the journals of her ancestor John Loveday; Mrs Penelope Hunting, who allowed me to make use of her doctoral thesis on Henry Clutton; the Duke of Westminster, who provided a photocopy of the Cliveden Visitors Book of the time his family lived there and gave me permission to reproduce paintings in his collection; the Earl of Orkney and the Countess of Sutherland, who gave their help with family papers; the staff of the Record Office at Aylesbury, where the National Trust has deposited a number of records relating to Cliveden; Angela Bolger of Soka Gakkai International, the owners of Taplow Court; Simon Howard, who allowed me to reproduce photographs in the Castle Howard archives; Kenneth Rose for suggestions and corrections to the Astor chapter; Philip Ward-Jackson for information on Lord Ronald Gower.

Thanks are due also to the Reverend Alan Dibden of St Nicholas, Taplow, for permission to reproduce the Orkney coffin plates; Rupert Maas for information regarding the painting by Augustus Egg, *The Life of Buckingham*; Oxford University Press for permission to quote from the articles in *Music and Letters* (these articles are listed in the Bibliography and are by Dibdin, Fiske and Scott); Mark Amory who, as Michael Astor's literary executor, gave permission to quote from *Tribal Feeling*; Thomas Woodcock, Somerset Herald, for identification of the coats of arms; the Trustees of the National Library of Scotland for permission to quote from Lord Orkney's correspondence; the Director and University Librarian of the John Rylands University of Manchester for permission to quote from the Kirkwell – Piozzi correspondence; Macmillan London Ltd for permission to quote from Joyce Grenfell's *In Pleasant Places* about spending Christmas at Cliveden; Andrew Roberts for information about visitors to Cliveden in the 1930s.

Special thanks are due to the staff of the House of Lords Library for locating some of the books that I consulted; Christine Akehurst and Jenny Barry, who managed to decipher my hieroglyphics, and to their word processor, which eased the production of the numerous drafts; Liz Drury for her skilful editing; Philippa Lewis for her help with the picture research; John Meek and Jane MacAndrew of Toucan Books; my wife Sylvia for her support and encouragement; last, but not least, John Lewis and John Tham, Chairman and Managing Director of Cliveden plc, for their help and encouragement. This is by no means an exhaustive list and to anyone who is reading the book and has helped, please accept my thanks.

JAMES CRATHORNE
February 1995

Foreword

THE ASTOR FAMILY, living at Cliveden for nearly four generations,
had the longest tenure of any of the families that have occupied the house.
We were the seventh family to take up residence, and we carried on the
tradition of previous occupants of redesigning and rebuilding.
The house has been altered by a succession of incumbents, each adding
a part of his or her own personality, each adding a bit of history,
and that is what makes the house so interesting.
If there is one link between all of the families, it must be politics.
From the 2nd Duke of Buckingham onwards, Cliveden has been
a magnet for the politicians of the day.
Cliveden has played a part in the dramas of history: the wars in Europe
and, of course, the two great wars of the twentieth century. It has twice
been a hospital for the injured and suffered the pains of those times.
The house has also been a centre for the arts, for great writers and
composers. Its stud produced many victories on the Turf,
and its kitchens produced meals never to be forgotten.
To me, however, it is more than that. Cliveden was a magical home in
which to be brought up for the first quarter of my life. The magic was of
exploring the gardens or roaming the woods on our ponies.
But it was the house that was special. Cliveden has always had for me a
happy atmosphere. It welcomed you, and it still does so today.
It is a house in which to entertain, and to be entertained.

WILLIAM, 4TH VISCOUNT ASTOR

CHAPTER I

Duke of Buckingham

CLIVEDEN 1666–1687

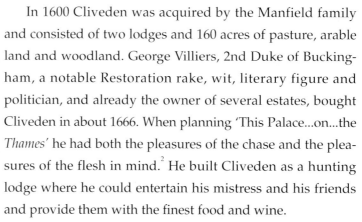

CLIFFDEN, Clifden, Cliefden, Clyveden, Cleveden or Cliveden, as it has variously been called over the centuries, takes its name from the steep chalk cliffs rising above the Thames that are broken by a wooded hollow and until the sixteenth century consisted of scrubland. In 1538 a description by John Leland ran: 'I saw a cliffy Ground as hanging over the *Tamise* and sum Busschis groinge on it.' He must have realized the potential of the site as he added, 'I conjectid that ther had beene sum site of an auncient Building.'[1]

In 1600 Cliveden was acquired by the Manfield family and consisted of two lodges and 160 acres of pasture, arable land and woodland. George Villiers, 2nd Duke of Buckingham, a notable Restoration rake, wit, literary figure and politician, and already the owner of several estates, bought Cliveden in about 1666. When planning 'This Palace...on...the *Thames*' he had both the pleasures of the chase and the pleasures of the flesh in mind.[2] He built Cliveden as a hunting lodge where he could entertain his mistress and his friends and provide them with the finest food and wine.

Buckingham positioned the house where the view down the Thames was at its most striking. At this point the ground sloped steeply, and massive amounts of earth were excavated and moved from the north side to the south side of the site. This created a 400-foot long 'step' on which the 25-foot wide terrace was placed, with the house in the centre. The different levels meant that the ground-floor entrance on the north side was a full storey above the

Right:
George Villiers,
2nd Duke of
Buckingham (1628-87),
a portrait by
Sir Peter Lely of c.1675.
Buckingham, courtier and
minister to Charles II, was
accounted by Dryden
'chymist, fiddler,
statesman, and buffoon'.
He bought Cliveden in
about 1666 and almost at
once began to make plans
for a grand house.

garden on the south. Thus was made one of the finest of all country-house settings and a *coup de théâtre* that predated the landscaping ideas of Capability Brown by a century. Today it seems natural enough to have built a house on high ground with a superb view, but to Buckingham's contemporaries it would have appeared somewhat eccentric – when the ideal was considered to be a sheltered situation close to water.

The building of Cliveden did indeed perplex a number of Buckingham's friends. Brian Fairfax, his agent and biographer, referred to Cliveden as 'that sort of architecture which Cicero calls *insanae substructiones'*.[3] John Evelyn, however, understood and admired Buckingham's achievement, and his diary entry of 22 July 1679 records, 'I went to *Clifden* that stupendious natural Rock, Wood & Prospect of the Duke of *Buckinghams*, & building of extraordinary Expense.' He continued:

> *...tis a romantic object, & the place alltogether answers the most poetical*
> *description that can be made of a solitude, precipice, prospects & whatever*
> *can contribute to a thing so very like their imaginations.*

Evelyn approved of both the view and the setting:

The house stands somewhat like Frascati *on the platforme is a circular
View of the uttmost verge of the Horison, which with the serpenting of the
Thames is admirably surprising... the* Cloisters, Descents, Gardens, &
avenue through the wood august & stately.[4]

A LIFE OF EXTRAVAGANCE AND INTRIGUE

Buckingham aroused every kind of emotion in those with whom he had dealings,
and his popularity and fortune ebbed and flowed. As described by Fairfax:

*For his person he was the glory of the age and any court wherever he came. Of
a most graceful and charming mien and behaviour: a strong, tall and active
body, all which gave a lustre to the ornaments of his mind; of an admirable
wit and excellent judgement; and had all other qualities of a gentleman.* [5]

But another contemporary, Bishop Burnet, held a somewhat different view:

*... pleasure, frolic, or extravagant diversion, was all that he laid to heart...
He had no steadiness nor conduct: he could keep no secret, nor execute any
design without spoiling it. He could never fix his thoughts, nor govern his
estate, though then the greatest in England.*

Burnet blamed Buckingham for the immoral behaviour of Charles II:

*... he had a great ascendent over him... the main blame of the King's ill
principles and bad morals was owing to the Duke of Buckingham.*[6]

For a time Buckingham was Charles II's most influential courtier and minister.
Their friendship arose from the friendship between their fathers. Following a
series of ennoblements, Charles I raised his favourite, George Villiers, to the
dukedom. Five years later, in 1628, the 1st Duke's meteoric career ended with
his assassination at Portsmouth by a discontented young officer. The King's
attention was drawn to the Duke's broken-hearted widow, who was with
child, and he assured her that he would be 'a father to her children and a husband to herself'. Thus it was that George Villiers, 2nd Duke of Buckingham,
and his brother Francis were brought up with the King's family, and at Trinity
College, Cambridge, their names were entered on the college books with that
of Prince Charles.

At the outbreak of the Civil War in 1642 the brothers, aged sixteen and fifteen, fought for the Royalist cause. Their mother remonstrated with the King,
who despatched the boys abroad, and they spent the next few years in Italy

*Charles II,
King from 1660 to 1685.
Until 1674 Buckingham
was a man of great
influence at the court of
the King.*

and France, 'where they lived in as great state as some of those sovereign princes'.[7] In 1648 they returned to England to rejoin the fight. Francis lost his life fighting with great courage at Kingston; George escaped to the Continent, but his houses and estates in London, Rutland, Essex, Lincolnshire, Leicestershire, Nottinghamshire, Buckinghamshire and Yorkshire, worth £25,000 a year, were confiscated by the Parliamentarians.

In 1649 Charles I was beheaded and his son Charles became king in exile. He was resolved on an expedition to Scotland, and Buckingham was the only English attendant permitted to remain with him on his arrival in that country. Some months later Charles and Buckingham came south and were crushed by Cromwell at the Battle of Worcester. Buckingham, thanks to his skill in disguise and mimicry, made his way to London, where he performed, unrecognized, as a mountebank for the amusement of the people. Later, he left the country for Rotterdam and remained on the Continent for the succeeding six years. In 1657 he returned to England, still in the hands of Cromwell and the Parliamentarians, with the intention of wooing the daughter of the Puritan Lord Fairfax, at one time Cromwell's commander-in-chief.

His keenness to marry Mary related to the fact that part of his sequestered estates had been given by Cromwell to Fairfax. He also believed that through Fairfax's influence he would obtain a pardon from Cromwell. At the time Mary was betrothed to Lord Chesterfield, but Buckingham's accomplishments, wit and good looks charmed both Fairfax and his daughter. Brian Fairfax (a cousin of Mary) explained:

> *The young lady could not resist his charms...*
> *All his trouble in wooing was,*
> *He came, saw, and conquered.*[8]

The marriage took place on 15 September 1657 at Bolton Percy church in Yorkshire. Angered by the marriage, Cromwell a year later, on a slender pretext, sent Buckingham to the Tower. Only Cromwell's death ten days later saved Buckingham from the block.

Although Cromwell's death led to his release from the Tower, Buckingham did not obtain his liberty until the abdication of Richard Cromwell in 1659. With the return of Charles II the following year Buckingham's star was in the ascendant. He became a Gentleman of the King's Bedchamber, carried the orb at the Coronation and was admitted to the Privy Council. The estates confiscated during the Commonwealth were restored to him, making him the

The Life of Buckingham *by the Victorian painter Augustus Egg, exhibited at the Royal Academy in 1855. The subject of this picture, supposedly set at Cliveden, is based on Alexander Pope's description of Buckingham in the third of his* Moral Essays, *published in the 1730s. Depicted here are the 'ridiculous pretensions', social and political, to which the poet made reference. It appears that the crown that forms part of the carved decoration of his chair is being placed on Buckingham's head. Charles II's arm rests on his shoulder, but the look on the King's face indicates that Buckingham's fall from royal favour is imminent. Other pairs of figures are engaged in private conversation, signifying the court intrigue that surrounded Buckingham's downfall.*

richest man in the kingdom. He became one of the gayest and most dissolute of the courtiers, and indulged in wild and lavish expenditure.

In 1666 two important, and costly, events occurred in Buckingham's life: Anna Maria, Countess of Shrewsbury, became his mistress and he bought the Cliveden estate. It is tempting to link these two events, as Alexander Pope did in the poem in which he described Buckingham as 'gallant and gay, in Cliveden's proud alcove, the bower of wanton Shrewsbury and love'.[9]

The worldly Buckingham, perhaps for the first time in his life, fell in love. A poem written to Anna Maria begins:

> *What a dull fool was I*
> *To think so gross a lie,*
> *As that I ever was in love before...*

And it ends:

> *Tis you alone, that can my heart subdue –*
> *To you alone it always shall be true!*[10]

Anna Maria had an extraordinary hold over the many men in her life. The gambler and libertine Count de Gramont explained:

> *As no person could boast of being the only one in her favour, so no person could complain of having been ill received.*[11]

Singling her out from among her contemporaries, Gramont wrote:

> *As for Lady Shrewsbury, she is conspicuous. I would wager she might have a man killed for her every day, and she would only hold her head the higher for it.*[12]

Two of her lovers, Henry Jermyn and Colonel Thomas Howard, did indeed fight a duel over her, and Jermyn's second was killed.

Anna Maria was Buckingham's acknowledged paramour for eight years, and it was during this period that the terrace at Cliveden was erected. George Vertue, that chronicler of artistic activity in the seventeenth century, recorded that William Winde was Buckingham's architect. Winde's family were Royalists who had found refuge in Holland, and William was born there. He returned to England at the Restoration to reclaim his family's lands. His principal interests in life were the army, in which he served, and military architecture. Buckingham's plan for creating the terrace at Cliveden required the type of

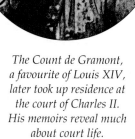

The Count de Gramont, a favourite of Louis XIV, later took up residence at the court of Charles II. His memoirs reveal much about court life.

Anna Maria, Countess of Shrewsbury, by Sir Peter Lely. Buckingham took the court beauty as his mistress in 1666 and probably built Cliveden for her.

earth-moving operations that were necessary for constructing the fortifications that Winde designed (later to be employed by him to create the terraces at Powis Castle in Wales). The terrace at Cliveden, with Winde's series of arcades running along the south front, was probably based on Mansart's great terraces at Saint Germain, which have a central double staircase of the same proportions.

The house was designed as a single block four storeys high. It was built in brick and had a hipped roof (similar in style to Ashdown House in Berkshire, which, almost certainly, was designed by Winde, as a hunting lodge for the Earl of Craven). The interiors of Winde's houses were handsomely fitted out. He used the finest craftsmen, who, as was the custom of the time, made their own designs for plasterwork, sculpture and woodwork. Winde also bought pictures and works of art for his clients and practised as a landscape gardener, laying out the grounds at Cliveden for Buckingham.

The paintings at Cliveden must have been of high quality. A catalogue of the 1st Duke of Buckingham's pictures (published in 1758) lists works by Titian, Tintoretto, Bassano, Veronese, Rubens, Leonardo da Vinci and Raphael. A number were smuggled out of the country by an old family servant called Traylman and provided the funds to support the 2nd Duke and his brother on the Continent during the Commonwealth. No doubt the Villiers coat of arms featured prominently throughout the house, as it did in Wallingford House, the Duke's London home.

During the time that Cliveden was being built, Buckingham would sometimes take both his wife and his mistress to the theatre. One such occasion, on 20 July 1667, was to have far-reaching consequences. By chance Harry Killigrew, one of Anna Maria's earlier lovers, was seated next to them. Killigrew picked a quarrel with the Duke and in the ensuing scuffle the

*An engraving of
the Duke of Buckingham
wearing the robes and insignia of
the Order of the Garter.*

18

Duchess of Buckingham fainted. Anna Maria took fright, Buckingham lost his blond periwig and Killigrew was wounded. Two months later Anna Maria took herself to a convent run by Benedictine nuns at Pontoise, near Paris. She was displeased that her husband had not challenged Killigrew after the humiliating incident at the theatre. The Earl of Shrewsbury felt that it was because of Buckingham that his wife had left the country and in January 1668 challenged Buckingham to a duel.

Charles II got wind of this and told the Duke of Albemarle to 'take security that he [Buckingham] should not do any such thing as fight'.[13] Albemarle misunderstood the instructions and waited for the King to inform him of Buckingham's movements, while the King, believing that Albemarle was watching the situation, thought no more of the matter. The duellists laid their plans unnoticed. Shrewsbury chose two relations as seconds, Sir John Talbot (one of Buckingham's bitterest enemies) and Bernard Howard, son of the Earl of Arundel. Buckingham decided on two experienced duellists, Sir Robert Holmes and Lieutenant William Jenkins.

On 21 January 1668 the duellists met at Barn Elms, near Putney Bridge. All the combatants engaged at the same moment in the French style of duelling, making it inevitable that at least one of the participants would be hurt. Howard 'ran furiously' upon Jenkins and killed him. Meanwhile, Robert Holmes wounded John Talbot in the arm – and both retired. Buckingham and Shrewsbury were now left to fight alone. By this time Buckingham had received a slight wound. He parried Shrewsbury's attacks, feinted and straightened his arm. His sword pierced Shrewsbury's right breast and came out at the shoulder. Buckingham drew away and returned to his house, and the wounded Shrewsbury was taken to Arundel House. The King, though very angry, spoke of 'the eminent service done by most of the persons... engaged' and, having talked about an extreme penalty in the event of a similar occurrence, pardoned all the participants. Pepys in his diary observed wryly:

> *This will make the world think that the King hath good counsillors about*
> *him, when the Duke of Buckingham, the greatest man about him, is a fel-*
> *low of no more sobriety than to fight about a whore.*[14]

Shrewsbury seemed to be recovering when on 16 March he died. Buckingham claimed that Shrewsbury had 'bin known to be an infirm and consumptive man long before and that this caused his death rather than the duel'.[15] Accounts of the duel became distorted in the retelling: Anna Maria, dressed as a pageboy, was said to have held Buckingham's horse, betraying no sign of emotion when her husband was mortally wounded by her lover, while Lord Peterborough's description was accepted up until this century:

> *All that morning she was trembling for her gallant, and wishing the death of her husband; and, after his fall 'tis said The Duke slept with her in his bloody shirt.*[16]

In truth, Anna Maria was still in France at the time of the duel. On her return she discovered that Sir John Talbot had taken control of her children and refused to release her a share of her husband's estate. She was barred from court and disowned by her friends and relatives. Turning to Buckingham, she was taken to Wallingford House. The Duchess protested, 'It was not for me and that other' to live together in the house, to which Buckingham replied, 'Why, Madam, I did think so; and therefore have ordered your coach to be ready to carry you to your father's.' This, commented Pepys, was 'A devilish speech, but they say, true; and my Lady Shrewsbury is there it seems.'[17]

As soon as the scandal began to die down, Buckingham attempted to restore himself in public esteem, and Pepys recorded him attending church with his wife, 'she patiently bearing with those faults in him which she could not remedy'.[18] As part of the process of gaining acceptance he bought from the Duke of Albemarle the Mastership of the Horse, the most important of all court appointments, for the considerable sum of £20,000.

In the spring of 1668 Anna Maria gave birth to a son, whom Buckingham acknowledged as his own. He gave the child the title Earl of Coventry, which had been conferred on the 1st Duke of Buckingham, and the King was persuaded to stand as godfather. The infant died five months later and Buckingham gave instructions that he should be buried in the family vault in Westminster Abbey. This was a reckless gesture. A mistress, however extravagantly and shamelessly entertained, was one thing, but the burial of a bastard in the family vault was quite another. The use of a hereditary title by an illegitimate child and the sanction of that title by the Abbey authorities implied that the Duke had taken upon himself the powers of the King. These factors would eventually weigh heavily against him.

If Buckingham's illegitimate son had lived, he probably would have inherited little but debt. The demands on Buckingham's fortune were great and included those of supporting Anna Maria and of the construction and running of Cliveden. His retainers appear to have been an unruly lot. On one occasion it was reported that 'the Duke of Buckingham's servants fought a set

A sword and the date 1668 set into the east lawn at Cliveden,
commemorating the duel fought by the Duke of Buckingham and the
Earl of Shrewsbury. The duel was fought on the Countess of Shrewsbury's
account, at Barn Elms, near Putney Bridge. Shrewsbury was wounded
and died some months later.

battle in his courtyard, Divers of them hurt, and the porter, it is thought, will
not recover'.[19] Another incident involved the elopement of a lady of quality
with one of his servants.

Buckingham enjoyed 'turning the night into day and the day into night'.[20]
The poet Edward Waller, having returned home at four in the morning after
dining with Buckingham and Anna Maria, declined an invitation for the following night, writing to his wife that 'such hours cannot be kept'. Another
occasion involving Waller was recorded by the city merchant Sir John Clayton, who wrote, 'never in all my life did I pass my day with such gusto, our
company being his grace, Mr Waller, Mr Surveyor Wren, and myself; nothing

Mary, Duchess of
Buckingham,
a portrait of 1659 from
the circle of
John Michael Wright.
The only daughter and
heiress of the Cromwellian
general Thomas Fairfax,
she married Buckingham
in 1657.
Ill-used by her husband,
she was known during his
lifetime as the 'Dowager'
Duchess; nonetheless, she
stood by him to the last.
The picture hangs at
Cliveden.

but the quintessence of wit and most excellent discourse.'[21] The quickness of
Buckingham's repartee and the accuracy of his verbal attacks on his enemies
was well known, Lord Ailesbury noting that the Duke 'would rather lose his
friend (nay the King) than his jest'.[22]

One of Buckingham's most famous 'jests' was his comedy *The Rehearsal*,
which was performed for the first time in 1671. The principal character, Mr
Bayes, the author-cum-manager who submits his play to the criticism of two
gentlemen, was a caricature of the Poet Laureate Dryden. Buckingham disliked Dryden's heroic rhyming dramas and personally coached the actor John
Lacey in Dryden's mannerisms and distinctive intonations to ensure that the
character of Mr Bayes was instantly recognizable. The play was a great success, and it is still occasionally performed to this day.

Dryden feigned indifference. He bided his time and some ten years later, in

1681, paid off old scores in his long satirical poem *Absalom and Achitophel*. This concerns the attempt by Lord Shaftesbury's opposition party to exclude Charles II's brother, the Catholic Duke of York, from the succession and to set Charles's Protestant illegitimate son, the Duke of Monmouth, in his place. It was written (at the suggestion of Charles II) at the time when Shaftesbury's success or failure hung in the balance, and was intended to influence the issue by showing under scriptural disguise the true characters of several of the political personages involved; chief among these were Monmouth (Absalom), Shaftesbury (the false tempter, Achitophel) and the Duke of Buckingham (the fickle Zimri). This is Dryden's brilliant description of Buckingham in the poem:

John Dryden,
*Poet Laureate and the butt
of Buckingham's comedy*
The Rehearsal,
first performed in 1671.

> *Some of their chiefs were princes in the land;*
> *In the first rank of these did Zimri stand:*
> *A man so various, that he seem'd to be*
> *Not one, but all mankind's epitome:*
> *Stiff in opinions, always in the wrong;*
> *Was every thing by starts, and nothing long;*
> *But, in the course of one revolving moon,*
> *Was chymist, fiddler, statesman, and buffoon:*
> *Then all for women, painting, rhiming, drinking,*
> *Besides ten thousand freaks that dy'd in thinking.*
> *Blest madman, who could every hour employ,*
> *With something new to wish, or to enjoy!*
> *Railing and praising were his usual themes;*
> *And both, to show his judgement, in extremes:*
> *So over violent, or over civil,*
> *That every man with him was God or Devil.*
> *In squandering wealth was his peculiar art:*
> *Nothing went unrewarded but desert.*
> *Beggar'd by fools, whom still he found too late;*
> *He had his jest, and they had his estate.*
> *He laugh'd himself from Court; then sought relief*
> *By forming parties, but could ne'er be chief:*
> *For spite of him the weight of business fell*
> *On Absalom and wise Achitophel:*
> *Thus, wicked but in will, of means bereft,*
> *He left not faction, but of that was left.*[23]

Dryden's poem was written when the Cabal had been in power for seven years. It was named for its principal members: Clifford, Arlington, Buckingham, Ashley and Lauderdale, who were a disparate and, by then, unpopular group.

BUCKINGHAM'S DECLINING FORTUNES

The House of Commons became increasingly dissatisfied with the Cabal for a number of reasons, which included the Secret Treaty of Dover and the alliance with France; the second Dutch War; and fear of a conspiracy to establish popery and introduce arbitrary government.

Lauderdale was the first to be driven from office, and Buckingham, who was never without his detractors, knew that he was likely to be the next. As Sir Gilbert Talbot wrote, he:

> ... personally courted all the Members in towne, the debauchees by drinking with them, the sober by grave and serious discourses, the pious by receiving the sacrament at Westminster... and because he is of opinion that the Parliament must have a sacrifice to appease them, his greatest endeavour with all men (next to the clearing of his owne innocency) is to caracterise the Lord Arlington for the most pernitious person in his Majestyes counsailes...

Sir Gilbert added:

> ... but I hope we shall spoile his designe, for we have a petition to be presented against him in the Lords House for the death of the Earl of Shrewsbury and the scandalous cohabitation with his wife, and at the same time an impeachment against him in our House for none of the meanest crimes.[24]

On 7 January 1674 the trustees of the young Earl of Shrewsbury presented a petition in the House of Lords – and on 13 January the Commons requested that Buckingham 'be removed from the King's presence and from his employment'.

The petition revealed the sad state of the thirteen-year-old Earl, who, 'as he grows in age and understanding, becomes every day more and more sensible of the deplorable death of his father, and of the dishonour caused to his family by the wicked and scandalous life led by George, Duke of Buckingham, with Anna Maria, Countess of Shrewsbury'. The petitioners continued that they would not have complained 'had the offenders employed the usual care to cover their guilt and shame', or had they given any 'outward show of remorse or amendment'. Instead, 'they ostentatiously persist in their shameless course of life, in defiance of the laws of God and man, having caused a

THE EPILOGUE TO TYRANNIC LOVE.
Originally spoken by Nell Gwynne (*vide* p. 148).
From Vol. ii of Buckingham's *Works* (1714).

THE APPARITION OF PALLAS.
The Rehearsal: Actus IV. Scæna I. (p. 51.).
From Vol. ii of Buckingham's *Works* (1714).

*Title page and
illustrations from the
1675 edition of
The Rehearsal.
The character of Mr Bayes
was a caricature of
Dryden, whose heroic
rhyming dramas
Buckingham disliked.*

base son of theirs to be buried in the Abbey church at Westminster, with all solemnities, under the title of Earl of Coventry'; and the petitioners ended with the request that their lordships should 'take the honour of the orphan peer under their protection'.[25]

The Lords ordered that copies of the petition be delivered to Buckingham and his mistress, who were required to give their answers in writing by the morning of 15 January. When the messengers came to Lady Shrewsbury's house with a copy and a summons, she had already left – perhaps for Clive-den. Buckingham's situation was decidedly uncomfortable, and he knew that the House of Lords could fine him heavily or send him to the Tower.

The ill-treated 'Dowager' Duchess of Buckingham (as she was unkindly known) showed how truly she loved and supported her husband by soliciting 'with the greatest passion, both for the Duke of Buckingham and my Lady Shrewsbury, that can be in the world'.[26]

Buckingham's answer to the Talbot petition was written in the third person. He began with a preamble admitting to the sins of the flesh, but contended:

It is generally known that the Countess of Shrewsbury parted from her husband because she thought her honour was not vindicated upon one who had done her a public and barbarous affront [Harry Killigrew]; that she went to Paris, and afterwards into a monastery, and that the Earl, upon a groundless jealousy of the Duke's having been the cause of her going away, was much incensed against him. He further answers that, after the death of the said Earl for which he professes to have a sensible grief as any of those gentlemen that subscribed the petition, the Countess, returning into England, and being disowned by her friends and relations, and the greatest part of her jointure injuriously kept from her, sent to the Duke to desire his assistance, which no man of honour could have denied a lady in her condition.[27]

BUCKINGHAM IS ACCUSED

On 14 January, at the moment his answer to the Talbot petition was being read out in the House of Lords, Buckingham was himself in the House of Commons answering a series of charges, both political and personal. He was variously accused of promoting popery, of speaking treasonable words against the King, of using his offices improperly to imprison the King's subjects, of charging money for exporting horses, of beating a man who asked him not to ride through a field of corn and even of attempted sodomy. Reference was also made to the death of the Earl of Shrewsbury and Buckingham's adultery. Buckingham, over a period of two days, answered all the charges, but to no avail. The Commons '*Resolved*, that an Address be presented to his Majesty, to remove the Duke of *Buckingham* from all his employments that are held during his Majesty's pleasure, and from his Presence and Councils for ever'. [28]

The pressure on Charles II to abandon his old friend was great, and he was now of the opinion that Buckingham was no longer of use to him politically. He summarily dismissed Buckingham from all his offices without compensation. For Buckingham, in his debt-ridden state, this was a severe blow, and only after a grovelling letter to Charles II was he allowed to sell his position as Master of the Horse.

Buckingham's answer to the Talbot petition was debated in the House of Lords on 31 January. The Duke 'acknowledged his fault and asked pardon of God and the House'. The Earl of Cardigan, Anna Maria's father, spoke of 'a letter of submission' from her and begged 'that she might not be made desperate'. [29] On 5 February the debate was resumed and the outcome was that Buckingham was ordered not to 'converse nor cohabit for the future'. To make certain this order was complied with the House required that both the Duke and the Countess should 'enter into security, by recognizance to the King in £10,000 each not to cohabit'.[30]

This extraordinary humiliation ended one of the most famous affairs of the seventeenth century. Anna Maria returned to her monastery near Pontoise, remarried three years later and died in 1702. Cliveden is perhaps the lasting monument to this 'Fatall Amour'.

POET, MUSICIAN AND CHEMIST

Buckingham wrote several poems about Anna Maria, and a couplet in *The Lost Mistress*, of 12 June 1675, reveals his feelings for her:

> *She had the power to make my bliss or woe,*
> *And she has given my heart its mortal blow.*[31]

His enforced separation from Anna Maria was marked by an excess of public piety and by constant attendance on his wife. He spent the next two years on his country estates, much of the time at Cliveden so as to be near the court in the event of his being recalled – but this never happened. He hunted all the winter and in the summer occupied himself with music and writing and chemistry. Throughout his life he spent large sums of money seeking the Philosophers' Stone (the hypothetical substance that, according to the alchemists, would convert all base metals into gold). He took his laboratory from place to place and would certainly have had it installed at Cliveden. His researches into the mysteries of chemistry were not entirely in vain. 'If he did not find out the philosophers' stone, he knew a way of dissolving or evaporating gold and other metals quicker than any other man of that age.'[32]

In 1663 he founded a glasshouse, which prospered for many years. In 1676 Evelyn visited this establishment and was delighted by 'the huge *vasas* of metall as cleare & pondrous & thick as Chrystal, also *looking glasses* far larger & better than any that come from *Venice*.'[33] Presumably a number of these were hung at Cliveden.

Another of his occupations was the breeding of carp. He wrote two letters from Cliveden to his friend the poet and rake the Earl of Rochester. In the first, of August 1672, he advised:

> *That you must be sure to cleanse your pond very well and lett no fish be in*
> *it whatsoever, only two carpes, a male and a female; and then that the next*

John Evelyn, the diarist, visited Cliveden in 1679. Three years earlier he had inspected the glasshouse at Vauxhall founded by Buckingham.

yeare you must take them out of the pond and put them into another for
feare of theyre being eaten by Pykes; this ... will make them breed infinitely
and grow very fatt.[34]

In the second he wrote that he had sent him 'two of the civillest carpes that
ever I had to doe with'.[35]

In June 1677, when Buckingham was imprisoned in the Tower (for the last
time), he wrote to the King:

> *... there is a necessity of speaking to you immediately in order to your owne*
> *service, and it is necessary also that it bee done with all kinde of privacy,*
> *and therefore, you Sir, pray let this dull man doe it in his owne dull way.*

He went on to explain that:

> *... it is most certaine that a little mistake in my builders at Clifden may*
> *cost me above £10,000, because I shall certainly pull it downe againe if it*
> *be not to my owne mind.*[36]

Work was evidently still being carried out on the house, and it would be interesting to know what the problem was – or indeed if there was a problem at all.

Charles II granted Buckingham's request, and he made good use of his
two days as, shortly after returning to the Tower, he was released on the condition that he returned to Cliveden.

THE YORKSHIRE SQUIRE

After the death of Charles II in 1685, Buckingham felt there was little reason
to live near the court. He left Cliveden and London for good and went to live
at Helmsley Castle in Yorkshire, which he had inherited through his mother.

Having played all the parts attributed to him by Dryden, to the surprise
of his friends he added that of country squire. The playwright Sir George
Etherege wrote an entertaining letter on 21 November 1686 from Ratisbon in
Germany, where he was Ambassador:

> *Received the News of your Graces retiring into* Yorkshire, *and leading a*
> *sedate contemplative life there, with no less Astonishment that I should*
> *hear of his* Christian Majesty's *turning* Bendictine *monk... Who cou'd*
> *have ever prophesy'd that the Duke of* Buckingham, *who never vouch-*
> *safed his Embraces to any ordinary Beauty, wou'd ever condescend to sigh*
> *and languish for the Heiress apparent of a thatch'd Cottage in a straw*

Hat, flannel Petticoat, Stockings... and a Smock... Who could have believed that ...the most polished, refined Epicure of his Age, that had regaled himself with the most exquisite Wines of Italy, Greece *and* Spain, *would in the last Scene of Life debauch his Constitution in execrable* Yorkshire *Ale? And that He, who all his Life Time had either seen Princes his Play-Fellows or Companions, would submit to the nonsensical Chat and barbarous Language of Farmers and Higglers?* [37]

Buckingham abandoned court intrigue and the Philosophers' Stone for country life. The close and happy relationship that existed between Buckingham and the moorland farmers sprang from their enthusiastic pursuit of the fox. Buckingham was the first Master of Foxhounds of the Bilsdale, which claims to be the oldest hunt in the country, and no-one rode harder to hounds through the wonderful rough country of that area. To historians of the sport, Buckingham is considered one of the pioneers of fox hunting as practised today. A fragment of a Yorkshire song preserves the memory of those days:

> *Oh with the Duke of Buckingham*
> *And other noble gentlemen*
> *Oh but we had some fine hunting.* [38]

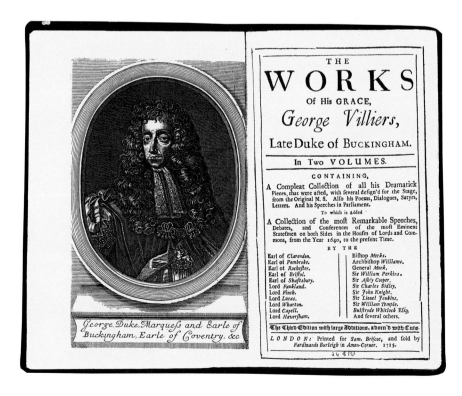

Frontispiece and title page of Buckingham's works, published in 1715, nearly thirty years after his death. In the volumes appear poetry written by Buckingham to his paramour Anna Maria, Countess of Shrewsbury.

29

*Pages from Buckingham's Commonplace Book,
which was about his person when he died.
In it he committed his innermost thoughts on
such subjects as love and lust.*

In April 1687 Buckingham caught a chill while watching a fox being dug out. He was put to bed in one of his tenant's houses in the market place at Kirkby Moorside. His condition grew steadily worse and he died on 16 April.

Alexander Pope in his *Moral Essays* (published in the 1730s) wrote a description of Buckingham's life and death. This has somewhat unfairly become his epitaph. Certainly the room in which he died was the best room available to this famous Master of Fox-hounds, known affectionately to his tenants as 'our Duke':

In the worst inn's worst room, with mat half-hung,
The floors of plaster, and the walls of dung,
On once a flock-bed, but repaired with straw,
With tape-tied curtains, never meant to draw,
The George and Garter dangling from that bed
Where tawdry yellow strove with dirty red,
Great Villiers lies – alas! how changed from him,
That life of pleasure and that soul of whim!
Gallant and gay, in Cliveden's proud alcove,
The bower of wanton Shrewsbury and love;
Or just as gay as council, in a ring
Of mimic statesmen and their merry king.
No wit to flatter, left of all his store!
No fool to laugh at, which he valued more.
There, victor of his health, or fortune, friends,
And fame, this lord of useless thousands ends! [39]

Alexander Pope,
whose Moral Essays
contained an unjust
account in verse of
the circumstances of
Buckingham's death at a
Yorkshire inn.

Buckingham died with a small commonplace book about his person. In it he recorded in verse his feelings about such matters as wives, mistresses, solitude – and death:

...a lasting sleep,
A quiet resting from all jealousy,
A thing we all pursue; I know besides
'Tis but the giving up a game which must be lost.

His feelings about his own life are perhaps summed up in the lines:

In those mighty volumes of the stars
There's writ no sadder story than my fate. [40]

Buckingham's body was embalmed, and on 7 June 1687 he was laid to rest in the family vault near his father and brother in Henry VII's Chapel in Westminster Abbey. The splendour of the service was greater than that held for Charles II.

Overleaf:
Golden carp and orfe in
the Water Garden at
Cliveden.

CHAPTER II

Earl of Orkney

CLIVEDEN 1696–1737

BUCKINGHAM'S ESTATES were sold or vested in trustees for the payment of his debts, and Cliveden was sold back to the Manfield family. Nine years later, on 28 October 1696, George Hamilton, 1st Earl of Orkney, bought Cliveden. He had been created an earl earlier in 1696 and in the previous year had acquired a wife, Elizabeth Villiers. The purchase of Cliveden perfectly complemented these events.

Elizabeth Villiers was Orkney's first cousin three times removed (as well as being the 2nd Duke of Buckingham's first cousin once removed). She had gone to The Hague as Maid of Honour to Princess Mary when the Princess married her cousin William of Orange. She had become William's only English mistress and remained so until Mary's death in 1694. The following year William arranged the marriage between Elizabeth and George Hamilton. William had settled nearly all the Irish estates of James II on her and within weeks of the marriage had raised her husband to the earldom.

Orkney became one of the most distinguished soldiers of the age and played a prominent part in the great battles of Queen Anne's reign. At Blenheim (1704) he commanded an infantry brigade under Marlborough and took 800 officers and 8,000 men prisoner. He also played a leading part in the subsequent battles of Ramillies (1706) and Malplaquet (1709).

Jonathan Swift described Orkney as 'An honest good natured gentleman', who 'has much distinguished himself as a soldier'.[1] A brother officer described him in October 1705 as 'sincere, but he is modest and is shy to medal'.[2] In a

Right:
George Hamilton,
1st Earl of Orkney,
(1666-1737), a copy by
Anthony Oakshett,
which hangs at Cliveden,
of a portrait by
Martin Maingau.
Orkney, who bought
Cliveden in 1696,
served under Marlborough
and fought at the battles of
Blenheim, Ramillies and
Malplaquet;
he became England's first
field marshal.

Elizabeth,
Countess of Orkney,
by Sir Godfrey Kneller.
Born Elizabeth Villiers,
she was a cousin of the
2nd Duke of
Buckingham.
Swift noted of this
portrait that the artist
had 'favoured her squint
admirably'.

memoir of him, Charles Dalton wrote:

> *As a general he was fitter to command a wing of any army than an army*
> *itself... He saw an immense deal of active service, and he won his high rank*
> *and position by his sterling qualities and personal bravery. William III*
> *had the most perfect confidence in him...*[3]

In February 1707 Orkney was elected one of the sixteen representative Peers
for Scotland in the first Parliament of Great Britain following the union of the
English and Scottish Parliaments. He was chosen to sit in seven successive

Parliaments from 1708 to 1737 and attended as frequently as his life in the army permitted. He was considered to be 'free from all party bias' and had considerable influence both in the House of Lords and at court. Like Buckingham, he found the situation of Cliveden ideal. Orkney's other honours and appointments included Knight of the Thistle on the revival of that order in 1704, Governor of Edinburgh Castle from 1714 to 1737 and Governor of Virginia from 1710 to 1737 (although he never visited America). From 1716 to 1727 he was also a Lord of the Bedchamber to George I.

A SQUINT LIKE A DRAGON

It was the power of the Countess's intellect rather than her beauty that made numerous men seek her counsel. The shrewd and cynical Swift described her in his *Journal to Stella* of 1712 as 'the wisest woman I ever saw'.[4] In 1713 Lady Orkney gave Swift a portrait of herself by Kneller, and Swift noted that the artist had 'favoured her squint admirably'.[5] In another letter Swift wrote:

> *Lady Orkney is making me a writing-table of her own contrivance, and a*
> *bed nightgown. She is perfectly kind, like a mother. I think the devil was in*
> *it the other day, that I should talk to her of an ugly squinting cousin of hers,*
> *and the poor lady herself, you know, squints like a dragon.*[6]

Lord Lansdowne, however, in his long poem *The Progress of Beauty*, was more flattering:

> *Villiers, for wisdom and deep judgement fam'd*
> *Of a high race, victorious beauty brings*
> *To grace our courts, and captivate our Kings.*[7]

Engraving of the Earl of Orkney, for whom numerous alterations and additions were made to the house and gardens.

From the moment the Orkneys bought Cliveden they became absorbed in plans to add to the house and gardens. Orkney was the fourth son of 'good Duchess Anne', Duchess of Hamilton in her own right, and this close-knit family wrote to each other regularly. The earliest surviving letter about Cliveden from Orkney, written to his brother Lord Archibald Hamilton on 11 January 1706, is of great interest. Orkney was worried by the fact that

> *I have got two old Houses [Cliveden and Taplow*
> *Court] upone my back... a good part of the Monney*

has been borrowed to buy it... tho I Haite the thought of paying Interest, and now to begine to build one needs a good purse.

Considering how best to alter Cliveden, he continued:

... the rooms are so high I dont like it, for ther is 3 Storys they tell me 18 foot high besids Garretts. We think of tacking away the Garretts and lowering the next story to the Garets [sic] which will tacke away near twenty foot of the Hight of the House and building a sort of wings like burely House [the recently completed Burley-on-the-Hill, Rutland] for offices... I am not as yet come to any resolutions about Cleavden and my head is turned with different opinions for not two men agrees, and I have had the opinion of sevrall of the chiefe men in England and one woud think it noe great mater since what is proposed is two little wings with a Colonaide to joine them to the great House.

Worried by the conflicting advice, he assured his brother:

I shall att last tacke my own fancy out of all. But now that I have some drafts and that I have had people there to see what it can be done for. I am more Embarassd for I find it will cost more than I expected.

In the same letter he recounted that the Duke of Marlborough:

... bid me get my whole desine and doe one part this Year and soe by degrees, but truly as for what Housing a desine I cant be with out any of it immediately, and the desine of tacking of the Roofe and lowering it I will find will cost a great dale and that must be done for I have noe necessity to have a 3d story 18 foot high.

It would seem that Orkney also intended to make alterations to the gardens:

... as for the Ground behind the House I have a plan how I shoud turn it but I see noe maner of Aperance of my doeing it as yet... [8]

Bronze bust of Thomas Archer, Orkney's architect, which stands in the West Wing Lobby at Cliveden. The bust was created by Anita Lafford in 1993 to celebrate the two-hundred-and-fiftieth anniversary of Archer's death.

The letter must have been written about the time that Orkney asked Thomas Archer to make plans to alter the house.

Archer reduced the height of the house by removing the hipped roof and attic storey and added wings on either side of the courtyard, joining them to the main house by quadrant colonnades. Orkney may have wished to add the wings to move the kitchen out of the main blocks, and a house between pavilions was very much the fashion of the day. 'This palace... is a noble building *a la moderne'*, as described by Macky in 1714.[9]

Thomas Archer's staircase in the West Wing. This is the only interior feature by Archer at Cliveden to survive.

Archer was a gentleman-architect who worked chiefly for members of the English nobility. He spent four years in Europe and became deeply interested in Roman Baroque: he was the first, and almost only, English architect to be greatly influenced by this style. In 1705 he obtained the court post of Groom Porter, which gave him control of gaming tables in the royal palaces and was reputed to be worth £1,000 a year. He probably owed this post to the Duke of Devonshire, who had employed him at Chatsworth. It is clear from the circle in which Archer moved that Orkney would have known him and perhaps met him at court. The engravings of Cliveden in the second volume of Colen Campbell's *Vitruvius Britannicus* of 1717 show the main building as altered for Orkney by Archer and the two wings that were added. Campbell wrote that Cliveden was:

> *...greatly improved and adorned by the present noble Patron, who after the dangerous Fatigues of thirty Campaigns, with immortal Honour to himself and Country, has now the Pleasure of this delightful Retreat, when the Business of his King and Country does not call for his Service... the Apartments are noble, richly furnished and commodious. Here is one of the most considerable Terraces in the Kingdom, being 24 foot above the Parterre and is as high as the level of Windsor Castle, and is 433 foot long, adorned with a curious Balustrade of Portland Stone; under the great Court in Front are arched Corridors that communicate from one side of the Offices to the other; a thing of great Use and Conveniency: The second and third Stories contain many fine Apartments magnificently furnished... The south front, with the fore-named Terrace; affords one of the most beautiful Prospects in the Kingdom.[10]*

Orkney spent much time and effort on the gardens, and the plan as it exists today is mainly the result of his vision. He wrote to his brother on 2 February 1706 explaining that there were:

The garden front of Cliveden as it appeared in Colen Campbell's
Vitruvius Britannicus *of 1717. The illustration shows William Winde's arcaded terrace built
for the Duke of Buckingham.*

*20 or 30 men att work ther and planting and other things doeing... I live
on a perfect Hurray of life, and when one has multiplicity of things in
ones head and that I dont accomplish them it gives the Splean, I am as yet
not Come to a resolution about Clivden but I hope pretty near upon paper,
but whether I realy goe on with it or not this Year I am Incertaine, for it
realy depends upon the purse.*[11]

Orkney sought the advice of Henry Wise, gardener to Queen Anne, and Charles
Bridgeman, later gardener to George I and George II. On 2 October 1723 he wrote
to one of his brothers about the Amphitheatre designed for him by Bridgeman:

*... the Amphitheatre is quite struck but wher to get turfe and trees for La
grand machine, besides ther is great difficulty to get the slope all that side of
the Hill where the precipice was, but Bridgeman mackes difficultys of
nothing I told him if I thought it had been the one Half of what I see it will
cost I believe I never had done it, he says the begining is the worst.*[12]

The Amphitheatre (now reduced in size) can still be seen, and numerous

The north front of Cliveden, an illustration from Vitruvius Britannicus.
Archer added the quadrant colonnades and wings to Buckingham's original house for
the Earl of Orkney.

entertainments have taken place there over the years.

Orkney commissioned several designs for a new parterre to replace the one that had probably been designed for him in about 1706 by Wise. The most ambitious and extravagant of these designs are two by Claude Desgots, who was the nephew of André Le Nôtre, and who succeeded him as Louis XIV's chief garden designer. Orkney may have met Desgots when he visited England in 1700 and designed the Maestricht Garden at Windsor for William III. Desgots wrote a memorandum advising on the planting of oaks, elms and chestnuts and the bordering of the parterre beds, not with the usual yews and hollies, but with flowering shrubs such as honeysuckle and syringa planted between each evergreen.

Orkney's aim in about 1713 seems to have been to enlarge the existing parterre. The final solution was quite simple, described by Orkney as his 'quaker' parterre. It comprised a rectangular grass sward 1,000 feet in length with a circle of turf at one end and bordered all round by a double row of elms. The work was probably carried out in the 1720s. The circular area survives and, according to tradition, Orkney's horses were exercised in this open-air manège.

Among the Orkneys' circle of friends was Pope, and he too offered advice

An account for £106 13s for the making of the Parterre at Cliveden.

about the gardens at Cliveden. In a letter dated 4 October 1736, he wrote to Orkney from his Villa in Twickenham:

> *I shall be good part of ye Winter in London, & there I can have the pleasure of planning & drawing Schemes, as well as of seeing and consulting yours, agst ye next Planting Season. We may so far enjoy Cliveden, inspite of bad weather; and it may have some merit, in sacrificing to the Place before I enjoy it.*[13]

In 1727 Orkney employed the Venetian architect Giacomo Leoni, who may well have been recommended to him by his friend and fellow general Lord Cobham, whose seat was Stowe in Buckinghamshire. Leoni produced designs that appear to be for the rebuilding of Cliveden in the Palladian style but, judging from the worry over finance, there must have been little chance of their being carried out. There are, however, two delightful buildings at Cliveden designed for Orkney by Leoni. The Blenheim Pavilion was built around 1727 and the Octagon Temple in 1735. Military trophies are carved on the Blenheim Pavilion, in the pediment and the spandrels of the arch below, and obelisks rest on cannon balls at either end of the parapet. Orkney also 'indulged the fancy of figuring the Battle of Blenheim, by the plantations of trees, now in full vigour.'[14]

The Octagon Temple is on the west side of the Parterre on the edge of the cliff above the Thames. Leoni produced four designs for Orkney to choose from, and the architect James Gibbs produced an alternative proposal for a temple of the same octagonal shape. Leoni wrote to Orkney on 20 June 1735 expressing the hope that he had given the carpenter 'suficient direction for ye framing of ye Cupollo'. As it was originally built, the Temple had a door on the east side facing the Parterre that led into a 'prospect room', of which Jeremiah Milles in 1742 recorded, 'ye ceiling is prettily done in fret work and ye architecture is not

View of the Amphitheatre created by Charles Bridgeman as it is today. Since Orkney's time the Amphitheatre has been the scene of numerous musical and dramatic entertainments.

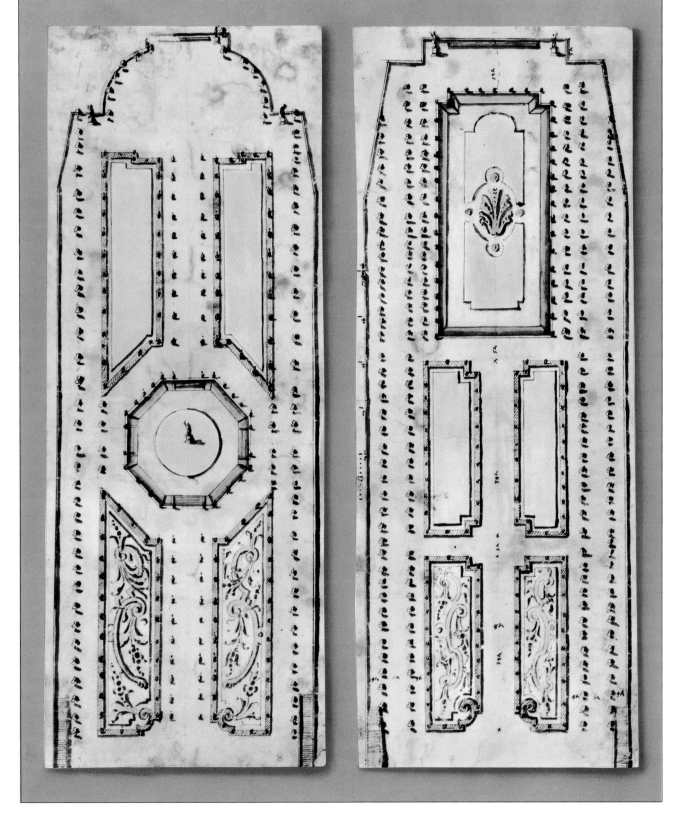

Two designs for a parterre at Cliveden sent to Orkney by Claude Desgots in 1713. Desgots, who was the nephew of Le Nôtre and his successor as Louis XIV's chief garden designer, came to England in 1700, when he designed a garden at Windsor for Orkney's friend William III. Desgots also sent Orkney a long memorandum giving advice about the planting of trees and the bordering of the parterre beds. Orkney commissioned several elaborate designs to alter and enlarge the Parterre but in the end settled for a simple rectangular grass sward, 1,000 feet in length, bordered by a double row of elms. He called this his 'quaker' parterre.

Design for a parterre, probably for Cliveden, by Henry Wise. When planning the gardens Orkney consulted Wise, who was gardener to Queen Anne.

amiss'. Beneath this, approached on the lower terrace walk on the west side, was 'a little cool room, by way of Grotto'.[15]

The enthusiastic traveller and diarist John Loveday rode from his home at Caversham on 10 October 1734 and recorded his approval of Orkney's alterations to the house:

> *There are 3 Stories to the grand front and 9 Windows in a Story; the Building seems full high for the width of it; it was surely monstrous before a 4th Story was taken down.*

Loveday also noted that 'the Trees in the Garden are forced to be upheld by Ropes, otherwise the Winds would tear them down.' Of the inside of the house, he wrote:

> *... most of the Rooms are wainscotted with Spanish Oak. Several have fret-work Cielings... The Stair-Case is very handsome, the Stairs are of Walnut-Tree and the Landing-Places are of Walnut-Tree inlaid.*

Paintings in the collection at that time included:

> *...the Earl of Orkney, and his elder brother the later Duke of Hamilton ... A Length of Prince Rupert, his Hair black and short, A Length of the Prince Elector Palatine; I take it to be Charles, elder brother of Rupert. A Length of the Duke of Northumberland. More Family Pieces A Length of Queen Anne, when Princess of Denmark. King William when a Child. The Earl of Pembroke with the golden key, the badge of his Office. A very good Head and Shoulders of Spencer the Poet. The Countess of Orkney had a lewd look. I know no Tapestry that excells Lord Orkney's; 'twas made at Brussels on purpose for him; the Colours are extremely lively, yet that is the least Commendation of the Arras...[16]*

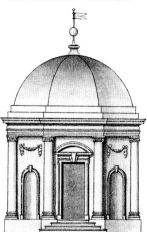

Designs by Leoni for the Octagon Temple.

The Octagon Temple, designed for Orkney by Giacomo Leoni in 1735. The Temple appears in the painting illustrated on pages 50-51.

The tapestries, commemorating Marlborough's victories, are similar to the set commissioned by the Duke at Blenheim Palace.

There was much entertaining at

The Octagon Temple, seen in Spring from across the Parterre. The upper part of the temple originally contained a 'Prospect-Room' entered through a pedimented doorcase from the Parterre, while under this was 'a little cool room by way of grotto' entered from the Lower Terrace Walk.

The Blenheim Pavilion, designed by Leoni and built around 1727. It celebrates Orkney's prominent role in the battle of Blenheim where he commanded a brigade.

Cliveden in the Earl's time – and one of the royal visitors was George I. The *London Gazette* for 7 September 1724 recorded:

> *...on the 5th instant the King dined at the Earl of Orkney's at Cleveden about seven miles from hence, [Windsor] attended by divers of the Nobility and Gentry. At His return hither in the evening, this Town was all illuminated, and he was received here with loud Acclamations of Joy; as he had been in the several Villages through which he passed.*[17]

Design by Leoni for the Blenheim Pavilion.

Five years later, on 30 July 1729, Queen Caroline and her son Frederick, Prince of Wales, visited Cliveden. The *Gloucester Journal* for 5 August 1729 reported: 'her majesty, the Prince of Wales, the Princess Royal and the Duke, were splendidly entertain'd at Dinner by the Earl of Orkney at his seat at Cliveden near Slough in Buckinghamshire.' Lady Orkney, however, was not satisfied with the manner of the Queen's reception and wrote to the Queen's Lady-in-waiting, Mrs Howard, on 5 August:

> *To have the queen doing us the honour to dine here, and nothing performed in the order it ought to have been! The stools which were set for*

*the royal family, though distinguished from ours, which I thought right...
put away by my Lord Grantham [Chamberlain to the Queen]... He
directed the tablecloth, that there must be two to cover the table; for he
used to have it so... The servants kept back the dinner too long for her
majesty after it was dished, and was set before the fire, and made it look
not well dressed, the Duke of Grafton saying there wanted a maitre
d'hotel. All this vexed my Lord Orkney so – he tells me, he hopes I will
never meddle more, if he could ever hope for the same honour... If you hear
of these mismanagements, pray be so good to say the house was too little
for the reception of the queen and so many great princes and princesses,
who, without flattery, cannot but be respectedly admired.*[18]

The Earl and Countess of Orkney had three daughters, all of whom grew up
at Cliveden. Anne, the eldest, eventually succeeded to the property and title.
It is often the case with Scottish titles that the eldest daughter succeeds in the
absence of a son, and in Orkney's case the warrant specified that the title
could pass through the female line, 'the heirs of his body whatsoever'.

The Countess of Orkney died in April 1733 and the Earl on 29 January 1737.
Three weeks before he died Orkney was honoured with the appointment of
England's first Field Marshal of 'all his Majesties forces'. He was buried in the
family vault in the grounds of Taplow Court, which was owned by the family
and marches with the Cliveden estate. At his request he was buried 'without
any funeral ostentation whatsoever'.[19]

*Brussels tapestries from
the* Art of War *series,
commemorating
Marlborough's victories,
hanging in the Great Hall
at Cliveden. They are
entitled* Embuscade,
Attaque *and*
Campement, *and they
were woven by Le Clerc
and Van der Borch from
cartoons by Lambert de
Hondt of c. 1710.
The borders are composed
of trophies of war with
Orkney's coat of arms in
the centre.*

*Coffin plate of Elizabeth,
Countess of Orkney, who
died in 1733.*

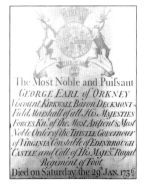

*Coffin plate of George,
Earl of Orkney. Both are
in Taplow church.*

*Overleaf:
View of Cliveden and the
Octagon Temple from the
south by an unknown
artist of the
mid-eighteenth century.*

CHAPTER III

Frederick, Prince of Wales

CLIVEDEN 1737–1751

W HEN Frederick, Prince of Wales, first visited Cliveden with his mother on 30 July 1729, as the guest of the Earl and Countess of Orkney, it was nine months after his arrival in England from Hanover. His links with the Orkney family were to develop through his friendship with the Earl's younger brother, Lord Archibald Hamilton, and his third wife, Jane. Frederick became captivated by Jane and, in spite of the fact that she had borne Lord Archibald ten children and was no beauty, she became his mistress. When Frederick married Princess Augusta of Saxe-Gotha, in 1736, Jane became Keeper of the Privy Purse, Lady of the Bedchamber and Mistress of the Robes.

In 1737 Augusta was expecting a child, and this prompted Frederick to look for a house in the country. His house at Kew was only a mile from his parents' house at Richmond, and his relations with them were deteriorating. The search led Frederick to Cliveden. Anne had recently succeeded her father, as Countess of Orkney in her own right, and had inherited the estate. Her husband, William O'Brien, 4th Earl of Inchiquin, was a supporter of Frederick and a frequent guest at his London dinner table; the Earl of Scarborough, husband of Anne's sister Frances, had worked as an equerry to Frederick and, in addition to these connections, Jane Hamilton was Anne's aunt. It was agreed that Anne and her husband should live at Taplow Court and lease Cliveden to Frederick. The rent was £600 a year. Thus Cliveden became Frederick's principal country residence. He must

Right:
Frederick, Prince of Wales (1707-51), *after Jean-Baptiste Van Loo; painted at Cliveden. Frederick leased Cliveden from Anne, 2nd Countess of Orkney, from 1737 until his death. The arrangement enabled the Prince to distance himself and his family from the King; great animosity existed between George II and his son.*

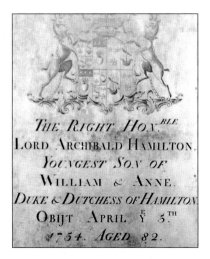

Lord Archibald Hamilton's coffin plate. His wife Jane was Frederick's mistress, and after the Prince's marriage Lady of the Bedchamber to Princess Augusta.

have moved in by July 1737 as the silversmith George Wickes submitted a bill at that date for an elaborate epergne and '2 rough cases to send them in to Clifden'.[1]

ROYAL ANTAGONISM

Relations between Frederick and his parents now went from bad to worse. In February 1737 Frederick had taken his fight with his father to have his allowance increased from £50,000 to £100,000 a year to Parliament and had lost. The Prince never showed any intention of living within his income and was already deeply in debt.

Later in the year came the drama of the birth of his eldest daughter, Augusta. Queen Caroline insisted that she would be present at the birth of her grandchild (partly because she doubted Frederick's ability to father a child). Frederick was determined to thwart her plans and did not tell his parents exactly when the baby was expected. The birth pangs started when Frederick and Augusta were with the King and Queen at Hampton Court. Secretly, and under cover of darkness, Frederick took the great risk of transporting his wife from Hampton Court to St James's Palace, where no preparations had been made. When the baby was born, Jane Hamilton was the only lady to witness the birth. The King and Queen were outraged, and the King sent his son a message on 10 September, eleven days after Augusta's birth, ordering him out of St James's Palace. Frederick had no alternative but to obey and took his family to Kew, then to Norfolk House in St James's and finally to Cliveden.

The animosity between Frederick and his father, George II, had also existed between George II and his father, George I. Frederick's birth in 1707 had brought little joy to his parents and, when his grandfather ascended the throne in 1714, his parents and sister

Princess Augusta after Jean-Baptiste Van Loo, the companion piece to the portrait of Frederick. Born Princess Augusta of Saxe-Gotha, she married Frederick in 1736.

View of Cliveden, c. 1750, by William Tompkins. Taplow Court is shown on the hill to the right of the picture. When Frederick took the lease of Cliveden, the Orkney family moved to Taplow Court.

came to England, leaving Frederick in Hanover. When Frederick eventually arrived in December 1728 he barely knew his parents or his six brothers and sisters. He was anxious to marry, but his father delayed finding him a suitable wife as marriage would give Frederick his own household and greater control of his own life. Seldom can a child have been more reviled by his parents.

On one occasion his mother, seeing Frederick crossing the courtyard at St James's Palace, said to Lord Hervey, 'that wretch! – that villain! – I wish the ground would open this moment and sink the monster to the lowest hole in hell', and there were other similar utterances.[2] Frederick's father was equally uncomplimentary about him, and after the saga of Augusta's birth the King issued a proclamation that anyone who visited the Prince of Wales would not be received at court. Queen Caroline announced that she never wanted to see her son again and she never did, though he attempted to visit her almost daily in St James's Palace during her final illness. She died, slowly and in agony, from a long hidden umbilical rupture.

Frederick and Augusta made Cliveden a family home, and eight of their children were born while they were living there. Frederick, unlike his father and grandfather, was fond of his family, delighting in his children; and, in spite of his acts of unfaithfulness, he loved his wife. She, in turn, was loyal and devoted. Frederick expressed his feelings for his wife in an ode he wrote to her. He loved her for:

> ... that gentleness of mind, that love.
> So kindly answering my desire;
> that grace with which you look and speak and move,
> That thus has set my soul on fire.[3]

At Cliveden, Frederick and his family enjoyed the house and the grounds, playing such games as cricket, which the Prince helped to popularize. The layout of the gardens was very much to Frederick's liking, and he instructed his head gardener, John Morris, to care for them as he had done in Lord Orkney's time. He may have been responsible for the planting of the Ilex Grove to the north of the house, in about 1747, and he asked his carpenter, George Warren, to enclose 'Two Great Arches for birds', which were presumably the arches at each end of William Winde's arcaded terrace.[4]

Frederick loved his adoptive country, and his affection for the common people ran counter to contemporary attitudes. He was the first member of the English royal family to mingle with his subjects, talking with them and sitting at their cottage tables. He took pleasure in visiting local inns, his favourite while at Cliveden being the Three Feathers (by the main gate; now the Feathers Inn), which was named in his honour.

He also enjoyed the company of writers and painters, especially if they did not support his father's Whig First Lord of the Treasury, Sir Robert Walpole. Pope, a staunch Tory and critic of George II, called Frederick a 'Champion of liberty' in his epilogue to the *Satires*, and he gave him a dog and a dog collar that bore the charming inscription:

> I am his highness' dog at Kew
> Pray tell me, sir, whose dog are you?

The Prince presented Pope with some urns for his garden at Twickenham, while Pope presented the Prince with four busts by Scheemakers of the great nationalistic poets, Spenser, Shakespeare, Dryden and Milton, for his library.

Frederick organized theatrical and musical performances in Bridgeman's amphitheatre, and on the terrace parterre. Sometimes he conducted the orchestra

The Music Party *by Philip Mercier, c. 1733. Frederick appointed Mercier his Principal Portrait Painter in 1729. This attractive and informal conversation piece hangs outside the French Dining Room. Frederick, a keen cellist, is shown with his sisters Anne, Caroline and Amelia. Two are playing the harpsichord and the mandora, and the third is holding a volume of Milton in her lap. A contemporary noted that this was probably the only time that Frederick and his sisters were 'in harmony'. The setting of the picture is the Dutch House at Kew.*

himself, and he composed music and played the cello with distinction. George II patronized Handel, and Lord Hervey remarked that 'An anti-Handelist was looked upon as an anti-courtier'.[5] This no doubt encouraged Frederick to support Handel's greatest rival, the Italian Bononcini. However, Frederick also admired Handel's work, attended his performances and, as his account books show, made payments to him for operas and oratorios.

The most famous musical event in the history of Cliveden was the first performance of 'Rule, Britannia'. On 1 August 1740 Frederick held a fête to commemorate the accession of his grandfather, George I, and celebrate the third birthday of his daughter, Augusta. The idea may have come from a fête held by George II on a visit to Hanover earlier in the year. Masques were still in fashion at that time for such entertainments. The Prince wished to impress his guests with his love of their country, and King Alfred was chosen as an appropriate subject for one of the masques. The reason for this is perfectly summed up in the inscription above the statue of Alfred in the Temple of British Worthies, built in 1733 at Stowe by Frederick's friend and political ally Lord Cobham:

Illustrated on the entrance ticket to the masque of Alfred, *the engraving after William Hogarth is of Hymen and Cupid and shows Cliveden in the background.*

THE MILDEST JUSTEST, MOST BENEFICENT OF KINGS;

WHO DROVE OUT THE DANES, SECURED THE SEAS, PROTECTED LEARNING;

ESTABLISH'D JURIES, CRUSH'D CORRUPTION, GUARDED LIBERTY;

AND WAS THE FOUNDER OF THE ENGLISH CONSTITUTION.

The finale of the masque of *Alfred* is:

> *Rule, Britannia, rules the waves:*
> *Britons never will be slaves.*

Thomas Arne composed the music of *Alfred*, and David Mallet and James Thomson wrote the lyrics. Arne was the leading figure in English theatrical music in the mid-eighteenth century and had composed a grand serenata, *Love and Glory,* in honour of Frederick's marriage. Mallet worked as Frederick's Under Secretary. He was a Scottish poet who, as Dr Johnson said, 'had talents enough to keep his literary reputation alive as long as he himself lived'. With him at Edinburgh University was the poet James Thomson,

A receipt from Frederick's account book of 1743 signed by Handel, signifying Frederick's patronage of the composer.

author of *The Seasons* and *Britannia*. He had dedicated his poem *Liberty* to the Prince of Wales in 1736, and shortly thereafter the Prince of Wales granted Thomson a pension of £100 a year. After Thomson's death, Mallet claimed that it was he alone who had written 'Rule, Britannia', but all the evidence suggests that this was not so. A report on the proceedings at Cliveden appeared in the *London Daily Post and General Advertiser* on Tuesday 5 August 1740:

> On Friday last was perform'd at Cliefden (by Comedians from both Theatres), before their Royal Highnesses the Prince and Princess of Wales, and a great Number of the Nobility and others, a Dramatic Masque call'd **Alfred**, written by Mr Thomson... The whole was exhibited upon a Theatre in the Garden compos'd of vegetables, and decorated with Festoons of Flowers, at the End of which was erected a Pavillion for their Royal Highnesses and the Prince and Princess of Wales, Prince George and Princess Augusta... Their Royal Highnesses were so well pleased with the whole Entertainment, that he commanded the same to be perform'd on Saturday last, with the Addition of some favourite Pantomime Scenes from Mr Rich's Entertainments, which was accordingly begun, but the Rain falling very heavy, oblig'd them to break off before it was half over; upon which his Royal Highness commanded them to finish the Masque of Alfred in the House.[6]

Thomas Arne, seen in this etching after Bartolozzi playing his score of 'Rule Britannia', which was performed for the first time on 1 August 1740 at Cliveden as the finale of the masque of Alfred.

The aria 'Rule, Britannia' met with the approval of those present on the day, and its popularity grew during the 1740s. Few composers have created such a stir with a piece of music extending to no more than a dozen bars. Handel borrowed it as the opening strain of his *Occasional Oratorio* six years later; Wagner said that the first eight notes embodied the whole character of the British nation and composed an overture based on it; Beethoven composed a set of variations on the tune; and it was used by Thomas Attwood in his *Coronation Anthem* and by Alexander Mackenzie in the overture *Britannia.*

The entertainment at Cliveden also included *The Judgement of Paris,* set to the music of Giuseppe Sammartini, the Prince of Wales's Director of Chamber Music, and a masque in one act written by Congreve. The scenes from Mr Rich's pantomime, mainly spoken in verse with a musical accompaniment, had splendid scenery.

ROYAL PATRON OF THE ARTS

Frederick's patronage in every area of the arts was formidable. He sat for nearly every portrait painter who achieved success during the period, and some seventy paintings of him, sometimes accompanied by members of his family, survive. As a collector, he saw himself as following in the footsteps of Charles I, and he also wished to emulate the collections of those who shared his political views, including Lord Cobham and Lord Lyttelton. His Old Master paintings were primarily Italian and Flemish works. The seventeenth-century Flemish masters such as Rubens and Van Dyck were particular favourites, and eight of the Van Dyck's that Frederick bought have remained in the Royal Collection, as have his superb drawings by Poussin and miniatures by Isaac Oliver. Frederick encouraged the arts in other ways as well and wished to help the founding of a royal academy. George Vertue recorded that Frederick spoke to him shortly before his death 'concerning settlement of an Academy for drawing and painting...' Vertue later

An invoice from Frederick's account book of 1742 for £32 11s for the making of two picture frames, from the frame-maker Paul Petit.

The Shooting Party *painted by James Wootton in 1740. Frederick, wearing the hunting livery and ribbon and star of the Order of the Garter, is seated. John Spencer, father of the 1st Earl Spencer, holds a partridge while the Duke of Queensberry, a gentleman to the bedchamber to Frederick, points into the distance. The invoice (left) relates to the magnificent frame for this picture, which was carved and gilded by Paul Petit for the Prince.*

wrote, 'No Prince since Charles I took so much pleasure nor observations on works of art or artists – and in all probability if he had lived, been an ornament to this country.'[7]

The Prince's taste in furniture inclined towards heavy pieces, fashioned walnut and mahogany and rich gilding. Much of his furniture was supplied by one of the most accomplished cabinet-makers of the day, Benjamin Goodison, whose work is characterized by large-scale carved decoration. His frame-maker was Paul Petit, who specialized in making elaborately carved and gilded frames. The designer William Kent worked for Frederick from 1732, and the best known of his creations for the Prince was a magnificent state barge that is now in the National Maritime Museum at Greenwich. The barge was manned by twelve watermen and a barge master. The oarsmen were elaborately dressed and wore large silver badges on their breasts designed by Paul de Lamerie. Frederick used the barge frequently, and sometimes musicians in another barge would accompany him.

THE HOUSEHOLD AT CLIVEDEN

Frederick and his wife lived well. Some of the bills of fare drawn up by Sir John Cust as Clerk of the Household to the Prince and Princess of Wales at Cliveden survive. To take just one day: on 5 September 1750 Frederick's supper consisted of 'Broth, Partridges fierst & Carbon' de al 'Italienne, Trotter Pye and Beignes, 1 Pullet and 4 Quails, Pease a la Creme and fleurons. Ragow Tongues Combs Eggs &c Proche, aux Ecrevisses, Patties en Salpicon'. The Lord of the Bed Chamber fared equally well with an entirely different menu: 'Veal Cutlets en papillotte, Tart creamd and Tartlets, 1 Duck, 2 pheas's po'ts & 4 Pidgeons, Artychoakes in Leaves, Perches anchovie Sauce, Chicks fracassead, Omelet Peaches & fritture'. The fare provided for the five-year-old Princess Elizabeth consisted of 'Loin Veal r't, 2 Chicks boil'd & sippits, French Beans, Peach Omelet, Currant Pudding baked'.[8]

For the entertainments on a grand scale at Cliveden it was necessary to hire some of the silver. On 17 December 1736, for instance, Wickes provided fifty-four candlesticks, twenty-six dozen knives, forks, and spoons, at a cost of £5.5s.0d. The expenses involved in running the Prince's household are recorded in his account books, and the nature of his household can be deduced by some of the job titles, among them, 'Gentleman usher of the Privy Chamber', and 'Servant to the pages of the Bedchamber'; there was even a 'Table coverer to the Gentleman of the Bedchamber'.

Gradually the highways were improving – and the time taken to travel between London and Cliveden was becoming shorter. One of Frederick's political allies, George Bubb Dodington, recorded in his diary for 6 November 1749:

Lord Bute, Mr Breton, and I went out from Carlton House, and arrived at Cliefden in three hours and twenty minutes. Met by the Earl of Inchiquin, Lord Bathurst, and Mr Masham. Followed by T R H [Their Royal Highnesses] Ladies Middlesex and Howe.[9]

Frederick would frequently lunch in London and dine at Cliveden – or vice versa – and on occasion set out for Cliveden as late as nine o'clock at night.

Frederick's famous state barge designed by William Kent on the Thames at Westminster, detail from a painting by William Scott. The twelve watermen were elaborately attired and wore silver badges designed by Paul de Lamerie.

THOUGHTS OF KINGSHIP

During the last decade of his life Frederick's youthful pranks and provocative behaviour were replaced by thoughts of the throne. His political energies had long been directed towards overthrowing Walpole, and he was at the centre of Whig opposition (attracting some of the Tories as well). Cliveden and other of his houses became the meeting place for such men as Bolingbroke, Chesterfield, Carteret, Wyndham, Cobham and George Lyttelton, who shared Frederick's political views. Walpole fell from power in 1742 and died three years later. This led to a partial reconciliation between Frederick and his father, and eventually to an increase in his allowance to £100,000 (the sum his father had received as Prince of Wales).

From 1747 Frederick was in constant discussion with political friends over what became known as the Carlton House Papers, through which he informed

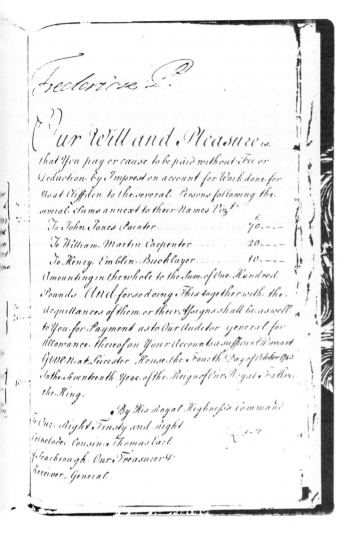

*Order of payment to be
made to the painter,
carpenter and bricklayer
at Cliveden dated
4 October 1743.
Frederick's signature
appears at the top of the
page.*

members of the 'opposition' as to what his policies would be when he succeeded his father. He declared his wish to investigate bribery and corruption in Government and to strengthen the militia, and claimed that he would need a smaller civil list than that enjoyed by his father. He was genuinely devoted to Britain, its people and institutions, and insisted on his family wearing clothing made only from British materials and of British design. He loved the English language and its literature, and objected to the use of German at court. He wanted above all to become the 'Patriot King', who ruled by consent, as described by Bolingbroke in his work of that name, and his first speech to Parliament as king was already written and ready to be delivered. Dodington in his diary made frequent reference to the work that went on in preparation for his accession. 'I din'd at Carlton House. The company only the Prince, the Earl of Egmont, and Dr Lee. The business, the immediate steps to be taken, upon the demise of the King...'[10]

During this period the powerful influence of James Stuart, 3rd Earl of Bute, made itself felt. Frederick had gone to Egham Races from Cliveden and heavy rain drove him to a tent. He decided to pass the time in a game of whist and asked an attendant to find him a congenial partner. Lord Bute was summoned and the ensuing game led to a close friendship with the Prince and Princess of Wales.

Frederick paid much attention to the upbringing of his children and was determined that they should be thoroughly English. One of the ways he achieved this was to involve them in amateur dramatics, and he ensured that the parts they played reinforced his ideals. In 1749 the eleven-year-old Prince George gave a performance as Porteous in Joseph Addison's *Cato*. Prince Edward, aged ten, was Juba, and Princess Augusta, aged twelve, and Princess Elizabeth, aged seven, also took part in the play. Their father and Lord Bute wrote a special prologue spoken by Prince George and an epilogue spoken by Prince Edward and Princess Augusta. In the course of the prologue Prince George declaimed:

What, though a boy! It may with pride be said,
A boy in England born – in England bred;
Where freedom well becomes the earlier state
For there the love of liberty's innate.

And in the epilogue Princess Augusta regretted that she would be required to wed some foreign royalty:

Could I have one of England's breeding.
But 'tis a point they're all agreed in,
that I must wed a foreigner.

To this Prince Edward added:

In England born, my inclination,
Like yours is wedded to the nation;
Indeed, I wish to serve this land
It is my father's strict command;
And none he ever gave will be
More cheerfully obeyed by me.[11]

Frederick had known nothing but hatred from his parents and most of his brothers and sisters, and his response was to devote much attention to his own children. Frederick's letters to Prince George are tender and encouraging:

You can't imagine how happy you made me yesterday, any mark of a
sincere, or a sensible, feeling heart gives me much more joy than any signs
of wit or improvement in your learning which I dare say will come also in
time. You have a father who loves you all tenderly...

In another letter written from Cliveden he exhorted the Princes to:

Take it by turns to tell me in writing once a week what you have read; it
will imprint it better on your mind and convince me that you both apply,
which will make me happy, as nothing can do that more, than a prospect,
to say my children turn out an honour to me and a blessing to my country.

Frederick, having chided George for his intermittent correspondence, ended:

You of all people should take more trouble, as God has given you so high a mark to govern one day so many nations, and if you do not please them, they won't please you in return. Read this carefully, and keep it as it comes from a father who (what is not usual) is your best friend.[12]

Frederick's establishment was by now almost a duplicate of the King's, and he had some two hundred paid posts either in his own household or connected with the management of the Duchy of Cornwall. It was, in effect, a government in waiting, and each post carried with it the prospect of future office.

George II's death seemed imminent, but before this Frederick himself died. His demise occurred on 20 March 1751 at Leicester House and the post mortem stated that the Prince had died of an abscess in the breast that had burst. It was widely believed that this had been caused by a blow from a cricket ball, sustained some time before, while playing with his sons at Cliveden. However, the immediate cause of his death seems to have been influenza, complicated by pneumonia. George II was playing cards with his current mistress when he received the news and he continued the game without comment. Later in the year he is said to have remarked, 'I have lost my eldest son, but I was glad of it'.[13]

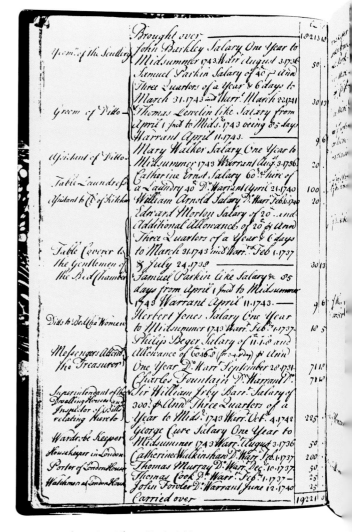

An extract from Frederick's accounts listing some of the specialist posts in the royal household. The total wage bill for the year 1742-3 was £26,305 14s.

George III, Frederick's eldest son. He spent his childhood at Cliveden and succeeded his grandfather to the throne in 1760.

EPITAPH TO A PRINCE

For many people Frederick's death was a tragedy. Lord Chesterfield was probably correct in describing the Prince in a letter to his son as 'more beloved for his affability and good nature, than esteemed for his steadiness and conduct'.[14]

He is remembered by an oft-quoted anonymous poem, which, although somewhat unfair to him, sums up the general antagonism to the Hanoverians that 'King Frederick' would perhaps have changed:

Here lies Fred.

Who was alive, and is dead.

Had it been his father,

I had much rather.

Had it been his brother,

Still better than another.

Had it been his sister,

No one would have missed her.

Had it been the whole generation,

Still better for the nation.

But since 'tis only Fred,

Who was alive, and is dead.

There's no more to be said.

In an alcove at Cliveden one of Frederick's biographers found the inscription:

Say, Frederick, fixed in a retreat like this,

Can ought be wanting to complete thy bliss?

Here, where the charms of Art with Nature join,

Each social, each domestic bliss is thine,

Thou shin'st in thy own virtues truly great,

By them exalted, with contempt look down

On all earth's pomps, except Britannia's crown.

   M.L.

Nov. 2nd 1749[15]

Frederick was denied 'Britannia's crown', but his son, as George III, became the only Hanoverian monarch who could be called a good and decent man. Part of the reason for this must surely have been because of the happy childhood days Prince George enjoyed at Cliveden, where his first lessons in the ways of kingship were taught to him by his affectionate father.

CHAPTER IV

Three Countesses of Orkney

CLIVEDEN 1751–1824

A FTER THE DEATH OF FREDERICK, Prince of Wales, his wife
Augusta gave up the lease and Anne, 2nd Countess of Orkney, and
her husband, the 4th Earl of Inchiquin, returned. In the following
decades Cliveden lost some of its lustre. Edward Gibbon, in his journal entry
for 18 April 1762, noted:

*This place... is very ill-kept. The Duke of York talks of
hiring it. They ask him £200 a year, but it would require
at least 140 more to keep the gardens in order.*

He did, however, enjoy the view from the terrace:

*From it you command a most glorious prospect of the
adjacent country, thro' which the Thames serpentines in a
manner on purpose for this house. From the terrace you
descend the side of a hill which are laid out with elegance,
and offer you at every turning prospects of another kind of beauty, less
extensive but more distinctly pleasing.*[1]

The Earl of Inchiquin was descended from the kings of Ireland and owned
land and property in the counties of Cork and Clare. He and Anne spent
much of their time there rather than at Cliveden. Anne died in 1756 and was
succeeded by her fifth child, Mary, her four sons having predeceased her.
Three years earlier Mary had married her first cousin, Murrough O'Brien,
who became the 5th Earl of Inchiquin on Mary's father's death in 1777. Mary,
like her brothers and sisters, was born deaf and dumb. Little is known

Right:
*Mary, 4th Countess of
Orkney (1755-1831),
a mezzotint after
Joshua Reynolds.
Mary succeeded to the
title and to the Cliveden
estate in 1790. This is
thought to be the only
instance of an earldom
passing through the
female line for three
successive generations.*

Anne, 2nd Countess of Orkney
(1696-1756), *to whom
the Orkney title passed on
the death of the 1st Earl.*

William O'Brien, 4th Earl of Inchiquin,
*Anne's first cousin whom
she married in 1720. The portrait is by
William Hogarth.*

of Murrough and Mary's life together, but one story is told of her approaching the cradle of her first-born child, to the great alarm of the nurse, armed with a large stone. She let the stone fall to the ground, and the child awoke, thus proving to the anxious mother that she had not inherited Mary's infirmity.[2]

Mary died in 1790 and was succeeded as 4th Countess of Orkney by her daughter – also called Mary. This is thought to be the only instance of an earldom passing through the female line for three successive generations. Mary married the Hon. Thomas FitzMaurice of Lleweni, Denbigh.

In 1795 Cliveden burned to the ground. Mrs Lybbe Powys wrote in her diary that the fire 'was caused by the carelessness of a servant turning down a bed. Very few items of value were saved. The loss is estimated at £50,000.' The Orkney tapestries were the most valuable items to be rescued. On 29 July Mrs Lybbe Powys visited the ruin and recorded her impressions:

We had all a curiosity to see the ruins of the once magnificent Clifden House, so we set off, and mounted a very steep hill; the whole fabric, except one wing, a scene of ruin – the flight of stone steps all fallen in pieces; but what seem'd the most unaccountable was, that the hall, which had fell in, and was a mass of stone pillars and bricks all in pieces, but two deal folding-doors not the least hurt, looking as if just painted! They were the entrance into the inner hall; an archway over them had fallen in. Poor Lady Orkney was then residing in the remaining wing.[3]

The Countess continued to live in the wings, now connected by a covered colonnade. She had plans to rebuild the central block of Cliveden, and an imposing design exists of around 1805 that has been attributed to John Nash and George Stanley Repton. It seems that the cost of rebuilding was prohibitive, and the central block was to remain a ruin for thirty years. However, in 1813 she built a gothick summer house near 'Cliefden's Spring' by the Thames. It was designed by Peter Nicholson, best known for his pioneering books on building methods.

Murrough O' Brien, 5th Earl of Inchiquin, *by George Knapton. He lived at Taplow Court and was a patron of the painter and diarist Joseph Farington, who wrote that Murrough's 'Open and Cheerful manner ... banishes reserve and makes every society into which He goes pleasant'. Knapton's painting hangs at Cliveden.*

THE MOST NOBLE MURROUGH O BRYEN MARQUIS of THOMOND EARL of INCHIQUIN BARON of BUREN of the KINGDOM of IRELAND BARON THOMOND of TAPLOW COURT BUCKS KNIGHT of the ORDER of St PATRICK. Died 10 Feby 1808. Aged 85 Years.

Coffin plate of Murrough O' Brien, 5th Earl of Inchiquin, created Marquess of Thomond in 1800.

71

FARINGTON AT TAPLOW COURT AND CLIVEDEN

In 1792 Mary's widowed father, Murrough, married Mary Palmer, niece and heiress of the painter Sir Joshua Reynolds, and they lived together at Taplow Court. Murrough was created Marquess of Thomond in 1800. He was an outgoing man and, according to the painter and diarist Joseph Farington, his 'Open and Cheerful manner ... banishes reserve and makes every society into which He goes pleasant'.[4] In the obituary notice in *The Gentleman's Magazine* in 1808 it was said that he was celebrated more as a 'Bon Vivant' than 'a fashionable', and for many years had the reputation of being a 'six-bottled man'.[5] His first toast of the evening was always to the ladies, and there would be a toast with each successive round of drinks. The final toast was always 'Merry be our Hearts'.

Farington recorded two royal visits to Taplow Court. The Prince of Wales dined with them in 1806, and on the other occasion the Queen dined and 'Lord Thomond stood the whole time behind Her Majesty's plate'. Farington spent much time with the Thomonds and was commissioned to paint several views of Cliveden and Taplow, which were later engraved. (A set of the engravings may be seen at Cliveden today.) On 15 September 1804 Farington and Sir Thomas Lawrence, President of the Royal Academy, were both staying at Taplow. Farington recorded the day spent together:

After breakfast Lord Thomond spoke to me alone, desiring that I wd. now fix upon a subject to make a picture of the size to be my own choice. – His Lordship and Lawrence walked with me to different points on the Cliff, & to the

The north front of Cliveden in the Countesses' time, shown in a coloured engraving of 1752 by John Donowell.

A watercolour of Cliveden in ruins. Only the wings of the house survived the devastating fire of 1795. The fire was apparently caused by 'the carelessness of a servant'. Very few items of value were saved apart from the Orkney tapestries. Following the destruction of the main block, the wings of the house were occupied by members of the family.

River, where in a boat we examined several situations, and selected 3 or 4 points for consideration. – His Lordship then said there might be two pictures. Seeing a pretty groupe of children, Lawrence proposed to me to paint such a groupe in one of the pictures, as Smirke had painted in conjunction with me, and as a memento of our being here together, to which I readily agreed. – The weather was excessively hot. At 3 oClock we set off in the Sociable for Cliefden Spring, at the bottom of the Cliff abt. a mile & 1/2 from Taplow Court, where before 5 we sat down to dinner in a most beautiful Scene.[6]

Mary, 4th Countess of Orkney, had given birth to a son and heir in 1778, and John FitzMaurice was the first member of the family to take the 1st Earl of Orkney's courtesy title of Viscount Kirkwall. John became a Member of Parliament in 1802 and the same year became engaged to Miss Ormsby. Shortly before the wedding he met Anna Maria, eldest daughter of John, 1st Lord Blaquiere. Farington recorded:

Miss Ormsby is the Heiress of much of the Godolphin fortune, may claim the Barony of that name. She has a good figure, is modest & amiable, & will possess £8,000 a year. Such a match wd. have been a great acquisition to

An early nineteenth-century watercolour of a proposed design for the rebuilding of the garden front. It was not carried out as the cost of the rebuilding was prohibitive.

Lord K. – & every preparation was made for the marriage when His attention was drawn to Miss De B... whose father has taken a House in the neighbourhood with a view it was believed, to bring on a union with His Lordship. – It succeeded, and Miss Ormsby was pointedly neglected

for Miss De B... at a ball which took place a week or two before Lord K. was to have been married to Miss Ormsby.

The consequence of this union has been great disappointment & unhappiness to His Lordship's friends. Lady Orkney His mother has been obliged

View of Cliveden, *an aquatint by Joseph Stadler from a watercolour by Joseph Farington. This was number thirty-seven from the famous series* History of the River Thames, *1793–1796 produced by Farington and Stadler.*

to quit His Lordship's House, where with His Aunt, she was on a visit, & this rude behaviour of the young wife, whose fortune is to be only, £600.[7]

The marriage was an unhappy one; Anna Maria made enemies of all around her, including her mother. Anna Maria wrote to her friend Mrs Piozzi of

'Cliefden's Spring' *drawn by S. Ireland and engraved by S. Middiman, 25 May 1785. This was a popular meeting place for boating parties on the Thames.*

The Fishing Party, *attributed to Joseph Farington and John Hoppner. The painting shows Farington sketching on the Thames with friends, possibly members of the Orkney family.*

that mother who could go on her knees and tell me when I lay at the point of death, that if I did not consent to say I would marry Lord Kirkwall she would give me her malediction and never more see my face! – behold the effects of her rashness, and of my duty, love and obedience![8]

At the same time she wrote to her mother, painting a bleak picture of her situation, 'My husbands affections and protection withdrawn from me by the malice of enemies as unnatural as they are powerful.' She complained of both her mother's and sister's rejection of her and their continued friendship with her husband.

Of her sister, she wrote that 'unmoved she beheld my children torn from my

Viscountess Kirkwall and her Children Taking Drawing Lessons from Monsieur Bononi, a watercolour by Thomas Rowlandson. Viscountess Kirkwall was married to the heir to the Orkney title. The Kirkwalls' marriage was an unhappy one, and the Viscountess succeeded in alienating all about her, including her own family.

arms'. She was distraught about the separation from her children and in another letter to Mrs Piozzi wrote that the 'children have been entirely at Cliefden'.[9]

John FitzMaurice, Viscount Kirkwall, died in 1820 without inheriting the earldom, as his mother outlived him by eleven years. His son Thomas, born in 1803, inherited the viscountcy on his father's death and would succeed to the Orkney title on the death of his grandmother in 1831.

On 10 July 1821 the 'Cliefden Estate comprising 380 acres, the site of the ancient mansion with the two entire wings, the noble terrace, The Temple, Pavilion and Banqueting-house... and other ornamental buildings' were 'peremptorily sold by auction by Mr Squibb & Son' in five lots. The auction took place at

Thomas FitzMaurice, son of Lady Kirkwall, a portrait by Joshua Reynolds (he is probably shown on the right in the picture above). He became the 5th Earl of Orkney in 1831, on the death of his grandmother, by which time Cliveden had been sold.

DESCRIPTIVE PARTICULARS

AND

CONDITIONS OF SALE

Of that highly distinguished Property,

THE

CLIEFDEN ESTATE,

SITUATED

ON THE BANKS OF THE THAMES,

AT

TAPLOW,

IN THE COUNTY OF BUCKS;

COMPRISING

380 ACRES

OF

FREEHOLD AND TITHE-FREE LAND,

THE

Site of the Ancient Mansion,

WITH THE TWO ENTIRE WINGS,

Extensive Offices and Gardens, beautiful Woods and Pleasure Grounds;

THE NOBLE TERRACE,

The TEMPLE, PAVILION, AND BANQUETING-HOUSE,

AT THE MUCH-ADMIRED SPRING;

FISHERMAN'S COTTAGE, TWO SUBSTANTIAL LODGES,

And other Ornamental Buildings in the Park and Grounds:

WHICH

Will be Peremptorily Sold by Auction,

BY

MR. SQUIBB & SON,

(BY ORDER OF THE TRUSTEE FOR SALE,)

At GARRAWAY's COFFEE HOUSE, in 'Change Alley, Cornhill,

On TUESDAY, the 10th of JULY, 1821,

At Twelve o'Clock,

IN FIVE LOTS.

The Estate may be Viewed till the Sale, by application to Mr. Tyre, at Cliefden, of whom Particulars may be had; also of Mr. Wetton, at the Library, Maidenhead; of Messrs. Fladgate, Neeld, & Young, Solicitors, 12, Essex-street, Strand; of Messrs. J. and W. Lowe and Cowburn, Solicitors, Tanfield-court, Temple; at Garraway's; and of Mr. Squibb and Son, Saville-row, London.

Auction particulars of the sale of Cliveden in 1821 following the death of Viscount Kirkwall in the previous year.

Garraway's Coffee House in Cornhill, London.[10]

The date on the conveyance of Cliveden to Sir George Warrender was 2 August 1824. The conveyance had to be delayed under the terms of his great grandfather's will until Thomas came of age. Whether Warrender was a friend of the young Viscount Kirkwall prior to the sale is not known, but they certainly became friends as the Kirkwall's second son, born in 1828, was christened Henry Warrender Hamilton, and Sir George was one of the godparents.

CHAPTER V

Sir George Warrender

CLIVEDEN 1824–1849

SIR GEORGE WARRENDER was famous as one of the great *bon viveurs* of his age and was known to his friends as 'Sir Georgeous' or 'Sir Gorge Provender'. He inherited a considerable Edinburgh trading and property fortune on becoming 4th Baronet in 1799 at the age of seventeen. He married Anne Evelyn Boscawen, sister of the 1st Earl of Falmouth, in 1810, and she out-lived her husband by twenty-two years. There were no children of the marriage.

Sir George's purchase of Cliveden was celebrated in an anonymous satirical poem that begins:

> *Ye Guardian Spirits of these shades, rejoice!*
> *Nymphs, Fauns, and Dryads join in grateful voice!*
> *Hail the new Lord of this reclaimed domain,*
> *Who bears no flaunting mistress in his train,*
> *Nor sighs for former joys which revelled here,*
> *When lust and riot led their mad career,*
> *When CHARLES'S courtiers woo'd their lawless loves,*
> *And Haughty VILLIERS ruled these classic groves;*[1]

Sir George commissioned William Burn to replace the burnt-out main block. Burn was an obvious choice of architect; his practice was based in Edinburgh, and country houses were by this time his speciality. Indeed, Warrender had already commissioned Burn to design Lochend House near Dunbar for him in 1823, and presumably started discussions with Burn shortly after Cliveden was conveyed to him in August 1824.

Burn played a central role in the transition of the country house from the

Right:
Sir George Warrender (1782 - 1849) painted in 1822 by Thomas Phillips. Sir George completed the purchase of Cliveden in 1824 and commissioned the Scottish architect William Burn to rebuild the burnt-out house. Sir George entertained lavishly in the rebuilt Cliveden, which soon regained the splendour of earlier days.

R.t HON.ble
IR G. WARRENDER B.t M.P.
ETATIS. SVE 40 A.D. 1822

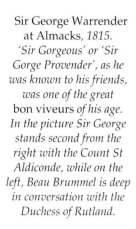

Sir George Warrender at Almacks, *1815. 'Sir Gorgeous' or 'Sir Gorge Provender', as he was known to his friends, was one of the great* bon viveurs *of his age. In the picture Sir George stands second from the right with the Count St Aldiconde, while on the left, Beau Brummel is deep in conversation with the Duchess of Rutland.*

formality of the eighteenth century to the comfortable asymmetry of the nineteenth. As well as designing new buildings, he successfully adapted such houses as Bowhill and Drumlanrig Castle, in Scotland, and Taplow Court, until shortly before part of the Cliveden estate. He was adept at reconciling the conflicting requirements of his clients for both grandeur and privacy with a convenient plan that included the segregation of the service quarters. Burn was restricted in his design for Cliveden by the existence of the two wings that had survived the fire thirty years before, and he had to use the foundations of the original central block on which to construct the new building. Burn's drawings for Cliveden are dated 1827 but, judging from letters, Sir George was already entertaining guests in his rebuilt mansion by that date.

SIR GEORGE AS HOST

Cliveden soon regained the splendour of its earlier days, and an invitation to Cliveden became much sought after. Sir George was a relaxed host: 'My rule is to say to my friends we dine at 7 we breakfast at 10 and all the rest of the time do as you please.'[2] The cuisine was of the highest order, as Mary Stanley recorded in a letter to Sir George:

> *I cannot tell you from how many I heard of your good living at Clifden; and Lord Cufeillis went home quite disgusted with his own chefs and full, as indeed we all were, of your Cordon Bleu...*[3]

Captain Gronow, that raconteur and student of manners of the period, remarked on one defect:

Sir George was a singular mixture of extravagance and economy, and though (for he was a renowned epicure) ... he fed his guests plentifully, the warming department was neglected, and the atmosphere of the dining-room resembled that of Nova Zembla.[4]

Four of Sir George's letter books survive. One, entitled *Autographs of Peers*, contains letters from ten dukes, ten marquesses, twenty-four earls, and countless other peers, many of them replies to invitations to visit Cliveden. Sir George clearly courted the aristocracy, but his circle of friends was wide. The Marquess of Downshire echoed the feelings of many when he wrote to Sir George, 'the site of your friendly paw does me good and thank you for the invitation'.[5]

Ascot week always was (and still is) one of the high points of the year at Cliveden. In 1828 the Marquess of Douro was upset when a change of plan meant that he could not join the party:

My only consolation in losing the pleasure of your hospitality, is that I am certain you will find it a convenience to have my place to give to one of those many who are desirous to see your castle, and meet the charming society you are known to have invited.[6]

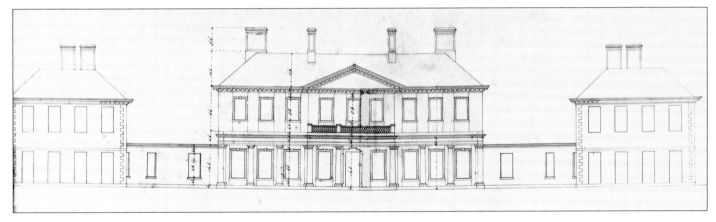

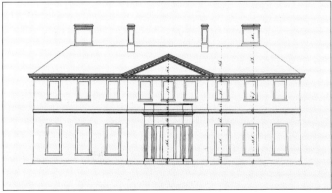

William Burn's designs for the north and south elevations of Cliveden. The drawings are dated 1827, but by this time the house was already in use.

Canning's Oak in the grounds of Cliveden. The tree was named after the statesman George Canning, who sat here and enjoyed the view down the Thames.

Right: A letter from Canning to Sir George asking if he might bring a young Etonian to lunch at Cliveden.

George Canning (who was Prime Minister for the last four months of his life) was a close friend of Warrender. In July 1826 he wrote a letter that begins 'My dear Sir G' (an informal greeting for the time). He was going to Cliveden to lunch and asked if he could bring a young relation from Eton with him. Canning's Oak (which must already have been fully grown in Canning's day) still stands at Cliveden. The statesman apparently spent several hours at a time sitting in contemplation under the tree looking down on the fine sweep of the river Thames below.

PATRONAGE AND POLITICS

Sir George was involved in politics for much of his life.

In 1807 he became Member of Parliament for Haddington Burghs, in his native Scotland, after a contest and on payment to Sir Hew Dalrymple of £4,500 for that parliament. The size of the payment meant that 'he was free to act as he pleased', but he gave 'very cordial support' to Sir Hew's friends in opposition.[7] He remained a Member of Parliament until 1832, representing successively Truro, Sandwich, Westbury and Honiton. He played an active role in the House of Commons and was a Lord of the Admiralty in Lord Liverpool's administration from 1810 to 1822. Charles Bagot commented, 'How prodigiously Warrender speaks in the House. He goes wallowing and spouting through all the naval questions like a great grampus.'[8] However, John Croker, another of his contemporaries, said of Sir George that he was 'a much cleverer fellow than he was generally thought'.[9]

Politics were still a matter of patronage, and Warrender's patronage was of particular importance in Scotland. Viscount Palmerston (later Prime Minister) wrote on 20 November 1832:

> *My Dear Warrender*
>
> *Though you have resolved to go and amuse yourself in Italy instead of taking care of the affairs of the nations in Parliament, I am sure you will let me ask you to do a public good, and to me a personal favour, by giving your support in Roxburghshire to George Elliot, in whose success I take great interest not merely as a colleague, but because he is one of the oldest friends I have and a very good fellow to boot. You really would oblige me very much if you could do this which I ask upon personal grounds and as a private friend and not as For.Sec [Foreign Secretary].*[10]

Visitors to Cliveden were not all politicians or aristocrats. The painter Sir Thomas Lawrence (who knew Cliveden from earlier days) gracefully declined Sir George's invitation of April 1829:

> *I feel very sincerely your kindness last night, in inviting me to your musick, and to have the honour of dining with you today. It is with no small reluctance that I now decline that invitation not I confess from any prior engagement, but simply because it is necessary for me to remain at home, and without the pleasurable excitement and comparatively late hours which the society at your house would certainly impose on one who has little power of limited enjoyment under such temptation.*[11]

With the advent of the railways it became possible to take the train from London to Maidenhead. Sir James Graham wrote in 1830, 'I shall come down by railroad... at Maidenhead I will get a chaise.'[12] The new rail link and improved roads made getting to Cliveden for one of Sir George's musical soirées both quicker and more comfortable.

Sir George was a competent musician and expected his guests to share his enthusiasm for music. He wrote in one of his letter books:

> *The English care little about music and in society talk when the finest compositions and most gifted singers are performing, it is ill mannered and on the Continent would not be, but fashion and not real good taste regulates all in London; however I did not fail to be severe on the noisy and whether it was a Prince of the Blood or a fine Lady, I always remonstrated and that failing did not invite the offending party next time.*

A good deal of Sir George's time was spent in Scotland, and on occasions he lent Cliveden to his friends. Lord Bedesley, thanking him for the loan of 'that charming place', offered some advice:

> *I heard you were going to send a housekeeper to Clifden and I think you will do well. Such a house wants a confidential servant to superintend were it only to see the windows opened at the proper times and well shut down at others. I have almost daily considered what should be done in the front of the house; and I shall be happy when we meet to give you the result of my meditations, but really the place is so enchanting, as it is, that one is inclined to fear any change might be for the worse. The place is very well kept and as we left it before the frosty nights the garden was still very bright. When I first went there it was in surpassing beauty.*[13]

No alterations were made to the grounds at Cliveden by Sir George, however, although a design for the Parterre of around 1830 shows that he was giving thought to the idea. It was created for him by Comte Alfred d'Orsay, artist, sculptor, collector and dandy, best known for his affair with his mother-in-law, the Countess of Blessington, during the 1830s and 1840s in London. The design, dividing the Parterre in four with a central fountain, fared no better than those produced a century earlier for the 1st Earl of Orkney, and it never went beyond the drawing board.

In August 1836 Sir George lent Cliveden to Queen Adelaide, wife of William IV. Earl Howe wrote after the visit:

> *The day was very fine. Your garden in the very highest order and beauty, and really your people did everything that could be most kind and attentive. We... walked for two hours about the grounds and all the party*

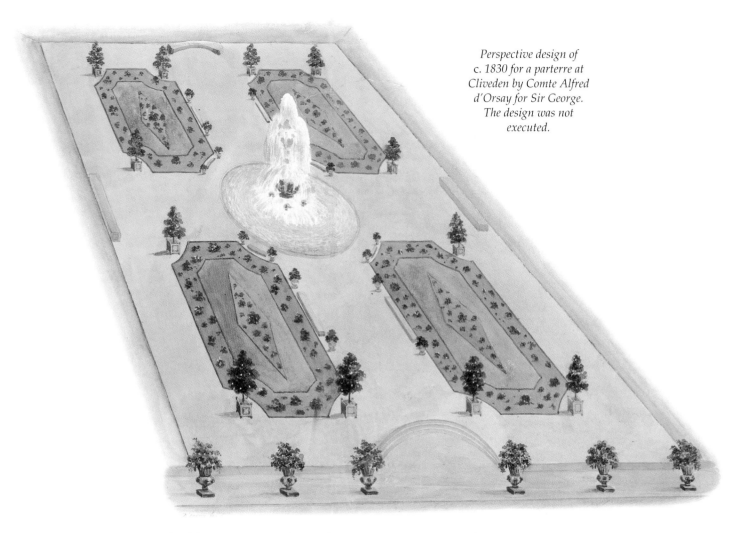

Perspective design of c. 1830 for a parterre at Cliveden by Comte Alfred d'Orsay for Sir George. The design was not executed.

left Clifden charmed with one of the most charming places they ever beheld – the Queen charged me to convey Her Majesty's thanks and to tell you of the pleasure she had from the visit.[14]

Sir George died on 21 February 1849 and was succeeded by his brother John, who later that year sold Cliveden to the Duke of Sutherland and the Duke gave it to his wife as a retreat from London. The selling price was £30,000. The Duchess's father, Lord Carlisle, noted in his diary on 20 June 1849 that Cliveden was 'a very enjoyable house'.[15]

The Thames at Cliveden
by George Arnold.
This shows the house
designed for Sir George
Warrender by Burn.
The picture hangs at
Cliveden and is one of
many works added to the
collection by the
proprietors of
Cliveden Hotel.

CHAPTER VI

Duke and Duchess of Sutherland

CLIVEDEN 1849–1868

CLIVEDEN'S NEW OWNERS, the Duchess of Sutherland and her husband, the 2nd Duke of Sutherland, owned vast estates in Scotland and Staffordshire. The Duke's grandfather, Granville Leveson-Gower, 1st Marquess of Stafford, had married as his second wife Lady Louisa Egerton. It was through her that their son was to inherit the Duke of Bridgewater's fortune and famous collection of paintings.

The son of the 1st Marquess increased the family's wealth by marrying a great heiress, Elizabeth, Countess of Sutherland in her own right. He succeeded his father in 1803 and received a dukedom in 1833, taking his wife's name as his title. (Thereafter she was known as the 'Duchess-Countess'.) When a few months later he died, Charles Greville described the 1st Duke of Sutherland as, 'a leviathan of wealth. I believe he is the richest individual who ever died'.[1] The land holdings of the 1st Duke comprised over a million acres in Sutherland, with land in Ross, Shropshire, Staffordshire and Yorkshire adding another quarter of a million acres – some 2,000 square miles in all. He is chiefly remembered for his controversial clearance policy in the Highlands.

In 1823 the 1st Duke's eldest son, Earl Gower, married Harriet Howard, third daughter of the Earl of Carlisle and his wife Georgiana (eldest daughter of the Duke of Devonshire). On 25 April 1823 a ball was given for the sixteen-year-old Harriet at Devonshire House in London. The Earl, then aged thirty-six, was captivated by his cousin (he had previously shown little interest in

George Granville
Leveson-Gower,
2nd Duke of Sutherland
(1786-1861), *a portrait
after John Partridge hanging at Cliveden. The Duke
commissioned Charles
Barry to design a new
house after a fire in 1849
destroyed the main block.*

marriage largely as a result of an earlier infatuation with the Queen of Prussia).
A week later, on 2 May, he proposed. On 21 May Harriet celebrated her seventeenth birthday and on 28 May the couple were married. Harriet was filled
with great *joie de vivre*, and from the time of their marriage they combined an
astonishing social life with much travel. Harriet's aunt, Lady Granville, wrote
of Lord Gower, 'as to his happiness, I never saw anything like it', and later in

the same letter she explained how Harriet's mother-in-law 'quite worships her; she says she has not the shadow of fault'.[2] They had eight children – including three daughters who all married dukes. Their fourth son, Lord Ronald Gower, was to write, 'Rarely, indeed, and in spite of a great difference of age, has that lottery of life turned out more happily than was the case in my parents' union.'[3]

The Gowers embarked on major building projects, beginning with Trentham Park in Staffordshire and Stafford House in London. Queen Victoria, on one of her many visits to Stafford House to attend a ball held by the Duchess, is reported to have said to her hostess, 'I have come from my house to your palace.'[4] Stafford House was a centre of social life in the capital, but more serious events took place there, too, including in 1853 the first meeting of the English ladies protesting against American slavery.

THE SECOND FIRE AT CLIVEDEN

Earl Gower succeeded his father as 2nd Duke of Sutherland in 1833. Shortly after the Duke and Duchess came to Cliveden in 1849, the main part of the house was again destroyed by fire. Thursday 15 November was a day of thanksgiving for the ending of a severe outbreak of cholera and the fire started in the morning, when the servants were at church. The Queen saw the smoke from Windsor Castle and immediately despatched fire engines to the scene; other neighbours also did what they could to help. *The Illustrated London News* of 24 November 1849 reported the details:

> *The family of the Duke of Sutherland were, at the time, in Scotland and the only persons in charge of the mansion when the unfortunate outbreak occurred were two female servants. The accident seems to have originated in the library, where some workmen had been employed until nearly ten O'Clock on Thursday morning week. The flames were first observed through the front windows of the mansion about one O'Clock p.m. on that day, by some persons near the spot, who hastened to the house and gave an alarm. Messengers were instantly despatched to Maidenhead, and in a very short period two engines arrived, but the fire had by that time attained so great a mastery that although an ample supply of water was at hand very little effect was produced upon the conflagration. The flames having communicated with the grand staircase, the whole of the upper floor of the main building was speedily on fire, and all hope of saving any portion of it*

during the progress of the work sundry other explanatory and constructive drawings.[7] The Duchess clearly enjoyed working with Clutton and told him 'how much satisfaction she derived from their consultations', and she instructed him to prepare drawings for 'alterations connected with the kitchens and stables'.[8] These alterations increased the need for a substantial water tower, as the volume of water pumped from the artesian well at White Place Farm on the other side of the Thames was no longer adequate. Barry had designed a clock tower for the Sutherlands at Trentham in 1840, and Clutton used this as the model for his tower at Cliveden. The project was put in jeopardy by the death of the Duke in 1861, but his heir agreed 'to gratify his mother by executing the work for her, as would have been the case had his father lived.'[9] The Water Tower became a monument to the 2nd Duke, and the date of his death was inscribed in the pediments.

The Water Tower designed by Henry Clutton, completed in 1861. The sculpture surmounting the tower is a version of the Spirit of Liberty *by Augustin Dumont, made for the July Column in the place de la Bastille, Paris.*

The Water Tower, completed in 1861 at a cost of £3,000, was the work of 'Victorian flamboyance and assertiveness'.[10] It is 100 feet high, the head laden with balconies, pediments and a clock face, and sculpture. The size of the head of the tower was dictated by the requirement for a water capacity of 15,000 gallons. At its top there is (as there was at Trentham) a version of Augustin Dumont's sculpture *Spirit of Liberty*, made for the column in the

An unexecuted design for a niche on the east face of the Water Tower for the statue of Prince Albert (right).

Prince Albert in Highland Dress in the grounds at Cliveden. The bronze sculpture, of 1865, is by William Theed the Younger.

place de la Bastille in Paris. An interesting feature is the projecting spiral staircase on the north side, which is derived from French domestic architecture and in particular from the staircase at Blois.

LORD RONALD GOWER'S DESCRIPTION

The Sutherland family's love of Cliveden is evident from the nostalgic description by their youngest son, the writer and sculptor Lord Ronald Gower:

Lord Ronald Gower was the youngest son of the 2nd Duke of Sutherland. This is the frontispiece to My Reminiscences, *in which Lord Ronald included many descriptions of Cliveden.*

> *Many happy days have we passed among these woods and on that river. The very name of Cliveden recalls the hawthorn and the may, the fields in June, the carpets of primroses and violets, the scent of the cowslips and the thyme, the hum of bees, and the music of the feathered choristers in the woods. Pleasant evenings were those when lingering on the river until the moon rose and warned us that it was time to leave boat and barge and climb the yew-tree path, through which the moonlight cast weird lights and shades. And when arrived above to pause a little on the old terrace, and watch star after star brighten in the deep purple vault of the summer night, listening to the far-away sounds from the river, to the cry of the men at the lock, as the belated boats returned to Maidenhead or Cookham, the laugh and the song fading slowly away over the water far below. And when all seemed at length hushed and still, to hear the rich, rare note of the nightingale bursting into music from out the great elms on the lawn beneath the terrace. And all the time the air perfumed from the great white globes of the magnolias and grape-like clusters of purple wisteria that climb the balustrades around.*[11]

Lord Ronald Gower's bronze statue of the Sutherlands' friend William Gladstone. His best-known sculpture is the Shakespeare Memorial at Stratford-upon-Avon.

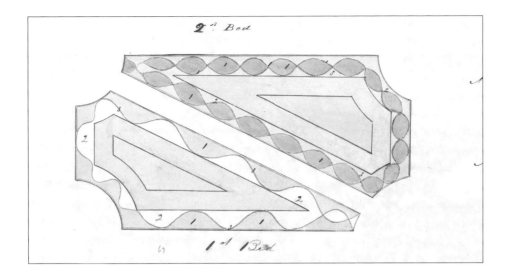

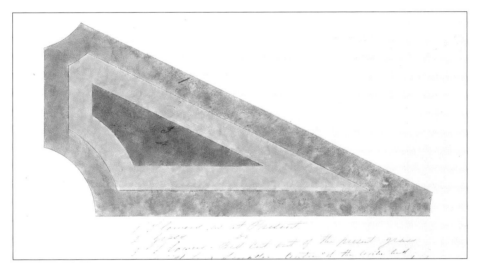

John Fleming's plans for planting the Parterre. Fleming, the Duchess's gardener, was one of the most influential garden planners of the day. The instructions for planting the two parterre beds above were: first bed, no.1 blue, 2 white, 3 line of Scarlet Geraniums; second bed, no.1 Scarlet Geraniums, 2 line of White Allysum, 3 Yellow Calceolarias.

JOHN FLEMING'S INNOVATIONS IN THE GARDEN

Lord Ronald recorded that, when the Sutherlands came to Cliveden, the Parterre was 'but a prairie':

> *... I remember our childish grief when the great waste of lawn was changed from a huge field of grass and wild flowers into its present state of trim sward flanked by stately flower-beds which Le Nôtre would not have despised, so dazzling were they in their summer hues. No one recalling its former state and its present can fail to admit that an improvement was made here by my mother.*[12]

The Duchess was helped in this task by John Fleming, one of the most influential gardeners of the nineteenth century. Fleming came to Cliveden in

1855, when he laid out the Parterre in its present form, and he remained there until his death in 1883.

Such was the success of the planting programmes he devised that his articles in the *Journal of Horticulture* were published in book form in 1864, as *Spring and Winter Flower Gardening Containing the System of Floral Decoration as Practised at Cliveden*.

The book was dedicated to the Duchess. His achievement was that he created a spring display to rival the standard summer display. He segregated plants by colour, preferring the strongest colours. In addition to tulips and hyacinths, his planting list included alyssum, anemones, arabis, daisies, crocuses, lily of the valley, cyclamen, snowdrops, gentians, ranun-culus, saxifrages, jonquils, scillas and pansies. Fleming wrote:

> As soon as the summer flowers are over, which is generally about the first week in October, the beds are prepared for the spring plants... The Tulips are first planted irregularly all over the bed, avoiding rows as much as possible; they are put in 6 or 7 inches deep... The other plants are then planted all over the surface as close as possible, both the Myosotis and Silene... When the time comes to remove these for the summer plants, the annuals are cleared away, and the Tulips taken out, as the footstalks will always show where the root is; the beds are then well hoed and raked over.[13]

The Parterre in the mid-nineteenth century showing Fleming's wedge-shaped beds.

The Parterre as it is today, seen from across the terrace. The shape of the beds remains as laid out by Fleming for the Sutherlands.

In 1868 Fleming planted a bed of different coloured sedums with the Duchess's monogram laid out in sempervivums and echeverias. This use of dwarf foliage plants caught the horticultural imagination and 'carpet-bedding', as it was dubbed, became enormously popular. It had the advantages of a long-lasting season, ease of maintenance and the more successful creation of patterns than could be achieved with flowering plants. By the 1890s it had become an international style, with patterned foliage beds in fashion across the world.

Fleming noted:

Each bed is over 80 yards round the outer edging... To fill the beds moderately it requires two thousand plants, and from six to eight hundred Tulips when well filled.[14]

The centre of each bed was planted with either rhododendrons or azaleas. All these were set well apart to allow for gladioli and hollyhocks during the summer. *The Gardener's Chronicle* of 6 June 1863 had this description of the end of the Parterre:

The connecting link between these two admirable series of beds at the point farthest from the mansion, is an immense circle with a grassy centre,

Far left: A nineteenth-century photograph of the hall before it was altered. In the niche stood the statue, Joan of Arc *by Princesse Marie-Christine d'Orléans, c. 1838. The encaustic tiles were a gift from Herbert Minton. Left:* Joan of Arc, *today set up in the Ilex Grove.*

encompassed with gay flowers, now broken here and there into masses by means of Honesty pegged down, and later in the season by Perilla, the intermediate colours during the spring being blue, red, white and yellow and in summer scarlet, white, and blue; the whole, when viewed from a distance, looking not unlike a gigantic broach of rich and varied colours set in a field of green.

Fleming's work was not confined to formal beds. In the 1860s he planted massed spring flowers in the woods, and on some of the banks the bluebells still rival in number the blades of grass. Fleming also landscaped a long shallow valley, where spring bulbs formed great splashes of colour, thus earning himself a place in the development of the wild garden.

During Fleming's time there were twenty-one hands employed to look after 250 acres. The work included tending the flower gardens, cultivating 5.5 acres of kitchen garden, as well as mowing 16 acres of grass often and 19.5 acres from time to time. Fleming's salary for overseeing this work was £100 a year.[15]

ALTERATIONS TO THE HOUSE

Left: Bluebell wood at the southern end of the estate, one of the glories of Cliveden in spring.

In the Sutherlands' time the interior of the house was very different from today. Prominently placed in the main hall was the life-size bronze of Joan of Arc by Princesse Marie Christine d'Orléans, and the floor was inlaid with encaustic tiles in a concentric pattern resembling an antique mosaic. These were a gift from Herbert Minton in recognition of the Sutherlands' patronage of his firm at Stoke-on-Trent, near Trentham Park.

Four Seasons
*on the stairwell ceiling by
the mural painter
Auguste Hervieu, 1855.
The Duchess's son and
three daughters appear as
the Seasons. This painting
is almost all that survives
of the Duchess's interior
decoration at Cliveden.*

The Duchess commissioned the mural painter Auguste Hervieu to paint portraits of her grandchildren in ovals, which were surrounded by a painted dense floral trellis. The Duchess also asked him to paint the *Four Seasons* on the stairwell ceiling. This is almost all that survives today of the Duchess's work at Cliveden. One commentator pointed out in the 17 November 1855 edition of the *Daily News* that the artist was:

> *notably assisted by his noble employer, who yielding to the impulse of maternal suggestions proposed that her son and her three daughters should, with the aid of the painter, personify the four periods of the year. The composition is very skilfully treated... Spring being impersonated by the Marchioness of Kildare; Summer by the Duchess of Argyle; Autumn, by Lady Blantyre and Winter, by the Marquis of Stafford who is*

represented in extreme youth. The figures, which are very well drawn, elegantly composed, and gracefully clad in drapery of appropriate colours are all accompanied with suitable attributes.[16]

The Library and its contents, which included fine editions of the French classics, were destroyed in the fire. The new bookcases were not marked in the usual way with numbers but with the names of plants carved in sycamore. Some of the furniture had been rescued from the fire – and additional purchases were made in London and Paris. The paintings did not rival the Sutherlands' superb collection at Stafford House, but works by artists such as Velazquez, Poussin and Canaletto appear in the inventory together with those of contemporary artists such as William Leighton Leitch, the Queen's drawing master, and Winterhalter. Contemporary sculptures by Albert-Ernest Carrier-Belleuse, John Lough and others completed the interiors.

GLADSTONE AT CLIVEDEN

Of all the great men who came to Cliveden, William Gladstone was the most welcome. He was one of the Duchess's 'best and greatest friends. Her admiration for him was boundless... His visits were always an intense pleasure, and even when she was suffering too much to receive others she would always make an effort to appear sufficiently well to receive him.'[17]

It was Gladstone who contributed the Latin words that 'made a very good frieze' on the entablature round the house.[18]

Starting on the north side and ending on the west, the four inscriptions translate as:

Constructed upon foundations laid long before by George Villiers Duke of Buckingham in Charles the Second's reign.

Completed in the year of Our Lord 1851 when Victoria had been Queen by God's grace for fourteen years.

Restored by George Duke of Sutherland and Harriet his wife on the site where two houses had previously been burnt down.

Built by the skill, devotion and design of the architect Charles Barry in 1851.

Mr Gladstone, *a* Vanity Fair *cartoon of 1869. Gladstone composed the Latin inscription on the entablature of the house.*

A reception given for Garibaldi by the Duchess of Sutherland in 1864.

The Sutherlands were among the most influential, as well as the wealthiest, of the great Whig families. Harriet was a powerful political patron, and Gladstone's success in Whig political circles of the 1860s owed much to her. The 'Cliveden Set' of the 1860s represented Whiggery at its most high-minded, and progressive, but political talk was no more important than discussions on religion or literature. Gladstone's diary shows how much he accomplished on his many visits to Cliveden. He noted the letters and speeches he wrote and the books he read. Typical entries are:

Saturday 4 June, 1859   *... off at 1 to Cliveden. We walked up from Maidenhead... Argyle read Tennyson aloud to us: very high strains indeed.*[19]

Saturday 26 May, 1860   *Off at 4 1/2 to Clifden: when we were received with the usual warmth...*[20]

Saturday 12 July, 1863   *... cabinet 2 1/2 – 4 1/4. Off to Cliveden by 5.5. Went to see Mr Mills magnificent collection of Sevres. Then calls: and ride. Read Les Miserables, Cliveden more beautiful than ever.*[21]

Saturday 2 April, 1864   *Conversation with A [Duke of Argyll] on future punishment. We had a delightful evening. Worked on budget.*[22] *[Gladstone delivered his eighth Budget on Thursday 7 April.]*

Saturday 23 April, 1864   *... off at 4 1/2 to Cliveden for the Garibaldi party there. After arriving took a skull on the river, from which he had just landed. An evg of great interest. Read – on utilitarianism.*[23]

GARIBALDI'S VISIT

The Italian patriot Giuseppe Garibaldi came to England in April 1864 as the guest of the Sutherlands' eldest son, the Marquess of Stafford. It was a visit that caused exceptional interest, and he was greeted with wild enthusiasm wherever he went. Before he left England he stayed with the Duchess at Cliveden. Lord Ronald recorded:

> *Never had he seemed more simple and likeable than during this quiet time, when he was no longer pursued by deputations and shoals of admirers and friends. One morning he was taken over the Home Farm at Windsor, and in the evening he was rowed on the Thames. The quiet and beauty of the spot called out the poetic vein that was strong in that glorious old buccaneer, and as he wandered amidst the beautiful glades and drives in Cliveden he repeated many an ode of Foscolo's and Filicaza's. He occupied the ground floor rooms of the left wing of the house, which open on a garden, all sunshine and flowers.*[24]

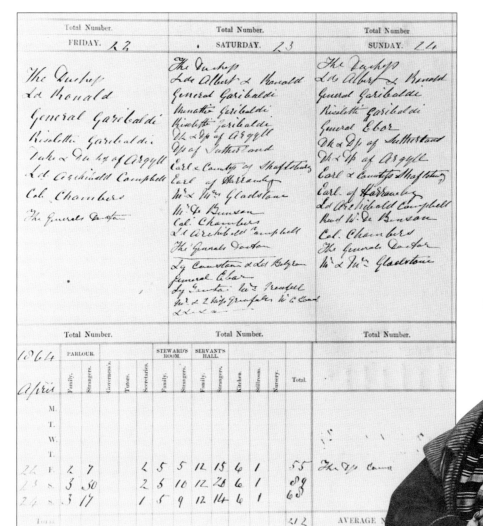

Right: The Sutherlands' day book for 22 to 24 April 1864 listing guests and visiting servants. Garibaldi was the principal guest and among the other visitors were Mr and Mrs Gladstone. Far right: Garibaldi at the time of his triumphal visit to London.

*The Garibaldi Room.
A photograph, taken in
1881, of the room occupied
by Garibaldi during his
stay at Cliveden in 1864.*

Garibaldi enjoyed Cliveden and the Thames, and 'The scene recalled to him some of the mighty river prospects of South America.'[25]

QUEEN VICTORIA AND THE SUTHERLANDS

Another very important friendship was that of the Duchess with Queen Victoria. On her accession in 1837 the Queen appointed Harriet Howard (as she then was) Mistress of the Robes, a post that she held when the Whigs were in office until her husband's death in 1861. The Queen in a letter to a friend explained that the Duchess was 'so anxious to do good, so liberal minded, so superior to prejudice, and so eager to learn, and improve herself and others'.[26] Indeed the Queen felt strongly enough about having Harriet at her side to cause the 'Bedchamber Crisis'. Lord Melbourne's Whig government resigned in May 1839, and when Sir Robert Peel accepted office, he requested that some of the Whig Ladies of the Bedchamber be replaced by Tories. Queen Victoria refused, Peel resigned and Melbourne was recalled. When Prince Albert died in 1861 (the same year as the Duke of Sutherland), the grief-stricken Queen chose the Duchess to be her sole companion for several weeks.

The Dining Room facing south and overlooking the Parterre, designed for the Sutherlands by Charles Barry.

Between 1854 and 1891 the Queen visited Cliveden on eight occasions. Her journal entry for 20 April 1854 gives a description of Cliveden shortly after work on the house was completed:

Immediately after luncheon we drove, (with the Ladies & Equerries in the next carriage) to Cliveden, where the dear Dss. of Sutherland, with the Argylls, Ronald & Elizabeth's 3 Children (the eldest boys & lovely little girl) received us at the door. The Duchess showed us all over the house, which is finished & being fast furnished. It is quite beautiful in strictly Italian style & the rooms so light and cheerful. They are arranged without actual splendour, but with all the Duchess's rare taste. In the Dining Room, beautifully painted flowers on a gold ground, intersect the pictures on the walls, the ceiling being painted through. The Duchess's Boudoir is quite lovely, a smaller corner room with a window over the chimney piece. The arched ceiling is painted to represent trellis work with creepers and

Queen Victoria, *a portrait drawing by David Wilkie that once belonged to Lord Ronald Gower.*

flowers on it, and has the effect of a bower. There are 4 panels painted with birds, & round Constance's picture is a wreath of pink & white roses, on a gold ground, which is quite beautiful. The rooms upstairs are also charming, such pretty wall papers & chintzes, all so well chosen.[27]

After the next visit she wrote in her journal:

I had not been there for about 3 years, when it was not quite finished. It is a perfection of a place first of all the view is so beautiful, & then the house is a "bijou" of taste... We drove with the Dss. & D of Argyll to a walk about the river, under the most splendid yew trees, 400 years old. Took tea in the Dining room – the prettiest of all, really quite beautiful.

In May 1866, the Duchess lent Cliveden to the Queen for ten days as the Queen wanted to be close to London during the Parliamentary battle over the second Reform Bill. The Queen had written to the Crown Prince of Prussia on 16 May:

The state of affairs being so critical I have been obliged to give up for the present going to my beloved Balmoral, which is a terrible annoyance to me as I require rest and quiet so very, very much. I am going to spend my poor sad birthday here and on the 26th we shall all go for 10 days to

The Library, as designed for the Sutherlands by Charles Barry. The room was later remodelled.

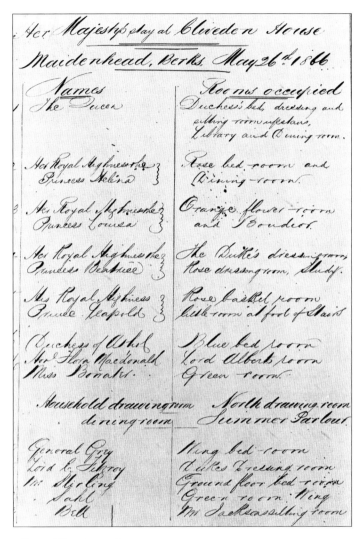

Queen Victoria was lent Cliveden for ten days in May and June 1866. The party comprised ninety people including her servant John Brown; they were accompanied by ten horses, twelve ponies and eight carriages.

Cliveden which the dear Duchess of Sutherland has kindly lent me, so that I shall be away from here during the noise and turmoil of Ascot.[28]

According to a letter written to the Duchess on 2 June, she found the peace and quiet she was looking for at Cliveden:

I wish again to tell you how comfortable & quiet we are here in this most beautiful spot wh. seems to be as quiet & primitive as if one was 200 miles from London. How <u>beautiful</u> the Woods are! We admire Burnham Beeches extremely, & Quarry Wood is also lovely, & the drives by Cookham, Marlow, Wooburn, etc. are quite like parts of Devonshire & parts remind me of the country about Coburg. I had <u>no</u> idea of the extreme beauty of the Country... I am constantly admiring the look of every thing here. Your gardener seems very intelligent and what a <u>nice</u> old Coachman you have got who kindly has shown us about everywhere. I have been able to sit out a great deal, wh. I always enjoy much.

Two days later she added:

I ought to have mentioned the other day, how very kind & attentive our Groom of the Chamber is, & how very kind & helpful he & every one is. Your little Piper plays very nicely... We shall all be quite sorry to leave this lovely place tomorrow, where we have been so quiet![29]

Queen Victoria's party at Cliveden consisted of ninety people, including eight policemen, two doctors, three dressers for the Queen and three for the princesses, and five footmen. The four children's education was not forgotten as they were accompanied by two governesses. In addition there were ten horses, twelve ponies and eight carriages. The Queen's piper was in attendance as was her servant John Brown, for many years after her

The Drawing Room, in the centre of the house, overlooking the Parterre, designed by Charles Barry. The double doors led to the Breakfast Room. This room has subsequently been remodelled five times. The furniture of the Sutherlands' house was supplied by Gillow, Hindley & Trollope, and by Morin of Paris.

husband's death her closest confidant. She brought two portraits of her beloved Albert and placed one on an easel at the foot of her bed and the much smaller one at the head of her bed. This depicted Albert asleep, as if he were lying beside her. Queen Victoria stayed in the Duchess's bedroom and used the Library as her sitting room.

The days were structured around the meals. Breakfast was at 9.30 a.m., luncheon at 2 p.m., tea at 5 p.m. and dinner at 8 p.m. Each day the Queen went for walks and rode in her carriage; she sat on the Terrace, reading or sketching. Some extracts from her journal conjure up a vivid picture of her stay:

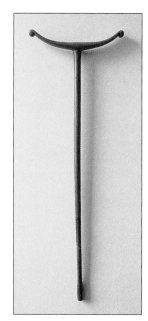

The stick used 'to push Harriet Duchess of Sutherland uphill from the River to the house'. It is in the West Wing.

> *27 May Breakfast below in the lovely dining room, which dearest Albert & I had so often admired together. – Very fine and very warm. – Walked with Lenchen in the beautiful shady walks, & drove along the riverside, through Taplow Park, which joins the Cliveden estate, in splendid woods just above the river. Then remained sitting out on the Terrace, & read Prayers & the Epistle & Gospel for the day. – Afternoon luncheon, writing etc. – Tea under the trees, after which took a very beautiful drive with Lenchen & Louise B. The 3 Ladies dined & the Dss. of Atholl read afterwards.*

28 May   A very fine warm morning. – Rode with the Dss. of Atholl along the river, where it was beautifully shady... Afterwards remained sitting out under the trees, writing which I always like, & which always does me good... I took tea on the terrace & afterwards a very pretty drive with the Dss. of Atholl, round by Maidenhead & on the opposite side of the river, from which the view of Cliveden woods is most beautiful, reminding me of Devonshire.

3 June   Service at 12, in the Dining room, performed by Mr Kingsley. Affie arrived directly after, having ridden over from Titness, where he is staying with Bertie & Alix. He remained talking with me & stayed till after luncheon. – Tea with Lenchen under the trees, then sketched, & drove till 1/2 p. 7. Very warm. The Dss. of Atholl, Ld. C. Fitzroy, & Mr Kingsley, who is very agreeable, dined, after which the Duchess read.

4 June   Breakfasted out on the leads. – Drove with Lenchen & Louise to a grass drive, where we all 3 planted trees, & then took a short drive & sat out reading & writing.

5 June   At a little past 5 left Cliveden where we passed a nice peaceful time.[30]

The final years of the Duchess's life were marred by ill health, and Garibaldi's visit in 1864 marked her last appearance in public. She walked with difficulty round the grounds at Cliveden and for the steep inclines was pushed with a specially designed stick with a curved section at one end that supported her. When she died in October 1868, the loss felt by her family and friends was overwhelming. Lord Ronald wrote, 'After her death, existence seemed to me a blank, and life lost for ever what makes life most precious and worth having.'[31]

On 28 October Gladstone wrote this moving entry in his diary:

The post brought a black-bordered letter which announced the death of the Dowager Duchess of Sutherland. I have lost in her from view the warmest and dearest friend, surely, that ever man had. Why this noble and tender spirit should have had such bounty for me and should have so freshened my advancing years, my absorbed and divided mind, I cannot tell. But I feel, strange as it might sound, ten years the older for her death... None will fill her place for me, nor for many worthier than I.[32]

Cliveden had always been the Duchess's house, and her son's family decided to sell it. The purchaser was her son-in-law, Earl Grosvenor, who had married her much-loved daughter, Constance.

Marble statue of the Duke of Sutherland by Matthew Noble, 1866. It is now positioned in the part of the grounds known as the Duke's Seat and can be seen from the terrace. The inscription on the plinth extols the Duke's virtues in Latin and English.

Overleaf:
The north front of Cliveden.
The porte-cochère was added by the Duke of Westminster in 1869.

CHAPTER VII

Duke of Westminster

CLIVEDEN 1868–1893

THE YEAR of the Duchess of Sutherland's death, 1868, 'the place was sold, and was luckily purchased by the Duke of Westminster, who, by acquiring it, saved Cliveden from the fate of falling into unworthy hands, or being cut up for building villas and hotels, forsooth!', as Lord Ronald Gower later recorded.[1] The 3rd Duke of Sutherland sold Cliveden to his brother-in-law, Hugh Lupus Grosvenor, Earl Grosvenor, who succeeded his

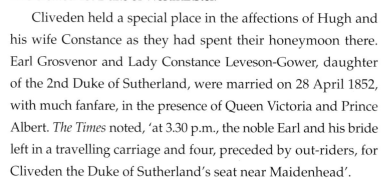

father as the 3rd Marquess of Westminster in 1869 and in 1874 was created 1st Duke of Westminster.

Cliveden held a special place in the affections of Hugh and his wife Constance as they had spent their honeymoon there. Earl Grosvenor and Lady Constance Leveson-Gower, daughter of the 2nd Duke of Sutherland, were married on 28 April 1852, with much fanfare, in the presence of Queen Victoria and Prince Albert. *The Times* noted, 'at 3.30 p.m., the noble Earl and his bride left in a travelling carriage and four, preceded by out-riders, for Cliveden the Duke of Sutherland's seat near Maidenhead'.

The couple spent two weeks at Cliveden, and during that time Constance wrote to her mother-in-law:

I must write to you a little line to tell you how happy I am and I think that my own darling husband is too... We had a delightful drive here and the place is so very pleasant after the bustle and excitement of London. We are both very flourishing and immensely happy.[2]

Queen Victoria was pleased with the match. She was delighted that 'dear

116

Hugh Lupus
Grosvenor, 1st Duke of
Westminster 1825-99.
*He bought Cliveden from
his brother-in-law, the 3rd
Duke of Sutherland,
in 1868. He was created
Duke of Westminster on
the advice of William Gladstone in 1874,
the year that this portrait
was painted by John
Everett Millais. The Duke
was a philanthropist,
patron of the Turf, lover of
pictures and enlightened
landlord. As* The Times
*noted, he 'could pass from a
racecourse to a missionary
meeting without incurring
the censure of even the
strictest'.*

Constance' had succeeded her mother Harriet, Duchess of Sutherland, as hostess at Cliveden and continued to visit the house:

> *I went up to see Constance, who was lying on her sofa, looking very handsome. She was confined three weeks ago and her little baby was brought in by her nurse for me to see.*[3]

The Queen visited again the following year, when Constance was 'daily expecting her confinement'. The Queen had 'tea and delicious fruit and walked a little in the lovely grounds'.[4] The confinements were frequent as Constance bore eleven children, of whom five boys and three girls survived infancy. Constance was beautiful and full of gaiety and the enjoyment of life. She made every party she gave or attended a success. Socially it was she who set the pace for her husband, who had more serious pursuits.

THE DUKE'S 'OVERPOWERING SENSE OF PUBLIC DUTY'

Hugh was a philanthropist, patron of the Turf, lover of pictures and enlightened landlord. He sat as a Liberal in the House of Commons and later in the House of Lords. He described his political beliefs thus: 'A Whig, in favour of free trade, will support principles of rational progress tempered with a spirit of moderation.'[5] This philosophy appealed to Gladstone, and their political association began in 1852, when Gladstone became Chancellor of the Exchequer. Mrs Gladstone's family were friends and neighbours of the Grosvenors, so the ties between them were those of neighbours as well as political allies. Another bond of friendship was, as we have seen, with Constance's mother.

During his first ministry Gladstone viewed the Marquess as one of his most valued supporters, even though he had always declined to accept ministerial office. On 17 February 1874, after his second term as Prime Minister had ended, Gladstone wrote: 'My dear Westminster, I have received authority from the Queen to place a Dukedom at your disposal and I hope you may accept it, for both you and Lady Westminster will wear it right nobly.'[6] The news was received with general approval. *The Morning Post* reported that 'the conferring of this important step in the peerage will be as popular as it is well deserved'.[7] As in the case of the dukedom of Sutherland, bestowed by William IV on the new Duke's grandfather-in-law, wealth and high regard rather than outstanding service were the criteria.

When Hugh succeeded his father as Marquess of Westminster, he inherited

*Constance, Duchess of
Westminster, and her husband,
the 1st Duke of Westminster.
They were married in 1852,
and the first part of their
honeymoon was spent at Cliveden.*

property, both settled and unsettled, valued at close to £5 million. The income from the London properties alone was £115,000 a year. At the time of his death in 1899 he was the richest man in the kingdom, but he regarded himself more as the head of a great public institution than a private millionaire. His efficiency in dealing with his affairs prompted a bishop to remark that he would rather have three minutes with the Duke than an hour with anyone else. Ironically, Hugh's father had been tight with money: 'He lived for the pleasure of getting money which he had not the heart to enjoy.'[8] As a result Hugh was frequently short of money, and he watched with increasing frustration his eventual inheritance growing larger and larger.

Hugh was widely liked and admired, and his 'extraordinary influence' was said to be in an 'overpowering sense of public duty'.[9] His life was described 'as one of the finest illustrations one beheld of what a nobleman should be'.[10]

The Westminsters' London home was Grosvenor House, and it provided a splendid setting for the large garden parties, dinner parties and balls that were a regular feature of the London season, when royalty and all the rank and fashion of the world were their guests. The Prince of Wales voiced a

119

Invoices addressed to His Grace the Duke of Westminster, dated 1893, from a gentleman's outfitter and an ironmonger in Maidenhead. The suit costing £3 15s. 0d. was ordered for Ben Cooper, the gamekeeper at Cliveden.

general feeling when he wrote, 'we always enjoy the entertainments you give at Grosvenor House so much'.[11] At Grosvenor House guests could enjoy Reynolds's portrait of Mrs Siddons and Gainsborough's *Blue Boy* and other famous works by such artists as Rembrandt, Van Dyck and Claude.

A notable meeting took place at Grosvenor House on 16 July 1894. The Duke was in the chair on this important occasion, when 'The National Trust for Places of Historic Interest and Natural Beauty' came into being. Later, in 1942, Cliveden was to be given to the National Trust.

The Westminsters' country seat was Eaton Hall, near Chester, set in 24,000 acres. The scale of the Eaton operation can be gathered from the fact that there were about eighty household staff, a hundred and sixty estate staff and forty gardeners. The Duke embarked on an extensive rebuilding programme at Eaton, which meant that for several years the family was unable to stay there. During these years Cliveden played a large part in the children's lives.

They loved being there, and for the parents and their friends it provided the perfect setting for parties for Royal Ascot each June, when fifteen to twenty guests would stay for the week.

The Duke was passionately interested in racing and, following in his grandfather's footsteps, created a stud that became one of the most successful in the history of the Turf. He was also a superb horseman and was for many years the Queen's Master of the Horse. His horses won many of the classic races, including the Derby four times. Bend'Or (named after the original heraldic description on the Grosvenor coat of arms *azure a bend or*) won the Derby in 1880 and was the sire of the horse of the century, Ormonde, winner in 1885 of the Derby, the Two Thousand Guineas and the St Leger. The Duke never placed a bet and, as *The Times* reported, he 'could pass from a racecourse to a missionary meeting without incurring the censure of even the strictest'.[12]

Although Cliveden was the smallest of the Westminsters' homes, thirty people were employed to look after the grounds and the farm that provided produce for the house. Careful records were kept in the Cliveden Dairy Journal, showing that the daily requirement was around three pounds of butter, forty-five pints of milk, five pints of cream and thirty eggs.[13]

The stable block, which borders the southern end of the Walled Garden, was designed by Henry Clutton for the Westminsters in 1870. This was restored by the Hotel in the early 1990s.

The Drawing Room, as altered by Henry Clutton for the Westminsters. The photograph was taken in 1889 and shows the effect of removing the wall separating the Breakfast Room and the Drawing Room. The illustration on page 112 shows Barry's original Drawing Room. The fireplace appears in both photographs.

THE WESTMINSTERS' ALTERATIONS TO THE HOUSE

The Westminsters were responsible for a number of alterations to Cliveden, employing Henry Clutton as the Sutherlands had done. In 1869 Clutton drew up plans for a number of internal changes, including turning the Breakfast Room and the Drawing Room at the front of the house into a single room. The only feature of the exterior not designed by Barry is the *porte-cochère* in the centre of the north front; Clutton was careful not to disturb the harmony of Barry's composition.

Clutton designed the stable block, including the open loggias either side of the Water Tower, and new boundary walls to the courtyard with gates and grilles. The stable block is an attractive, rather idiosyncratic, building, with a very individual form of dormer window breaking through the line of the parapet. Clutton was also involved in installing 'Bells, Warming Apparatus and Kitchen Fittings', offices in the East and West Wings and an extra loggia at the east side of the courtyard. On the opposite side of the Forecourt he designed a charming circular dovecote in red brick and timber with a tiled roof.

The Duchess of Westminster's Sitting Room. Over the mantelpiece hung a portrait of the Duchess's mother, the Duchess of Sutherland, which is a version of the portrait on page 93. The bisque porcelain figures on wall brackets, designed by Albert-Ernest Carrier-Belleuse and made by Minton, were created for the Westminsters' wedding banquet. Above them is a portrait of the Duke of Westminster.

A somewhat eccentric idea of the Westminsters was to encase the East and West Wings of the house in pink terracotta to a design in the Flemish Renaissance style by R. W. Edis. The design for the work on the East Wing is dated 1886, and only the East Wing was altered. This was returned to its original appearance by Cliveden's next owner.

THE LATER YEARS OF WESTMINSTER OWNERSHIP

The charmed life of Hugh and Constance Westminster came to an end in 1879, when her health began to decline. They had been married for twenty-seven years, and she was only forty-five when she fell victim to Bright's disease. The symptoms worsened, and the pain and sickness increased, but she was just well enough to go to Epsom with her husband to see Bend'Or win the Derby in the summer of 1880. She died before the end of the year, greatly mourned by her family and a great many friends.

Constance's death was not the only domestic tragedy that Hugh had to

The dovecote on the west side of the Forecourt, designed by Henry Clutton for the Westminsters.

bear. The health of his eldest son, the twenty-eight-year-old Earl Grosvenor, had been steadily deteriorating, and in February 1884 he died, leaving his four-year-old son (always known as Bend'Or) the heir to the dukedom.

Two years after Constance's death Hugh married Katherine Cavendish,

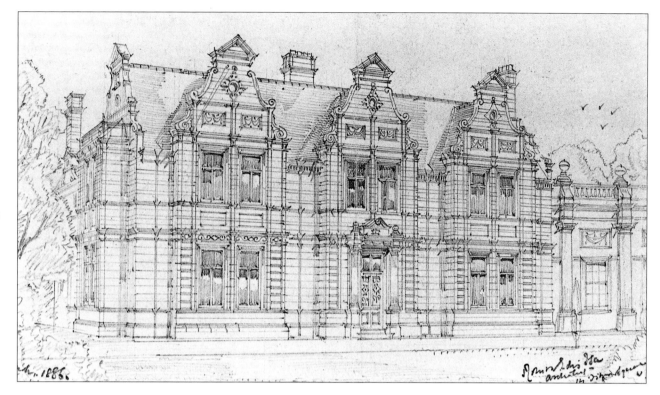

A perspective drawing of 1886 for the refacing of the East Wing by R. W. Edis, an eccentric design in the Flemish Renaissance style. The façade, finished in pink stucco, was superimposed on Barry's architecture. The first act of the next owner was to return the façade as near as possible to Barry's original.

daughter of the 2nd Lord Chesham. There was a thirty-two-year difference in their ages, but it was undoubtedly a love match. Katherine's position cannot have been an easy one, with three of her step-children not only older than her but already married with children of their own; there were other step-children who were her age, and the two youngest were still in the schoolroom. Her tact and good nature won the lifelong affection of all of them. She outlived her step-children and all but one of her own children, dying in 1941.

The Duke again had the happiness of seeing the nurseries of Eaton Hall, Cliveden and Grosvenor House filled with children of his own, as well as visiting grandchildren. The Duke and his second wife had two sons and two daughters, the present Duke of Westminster being descended from their youngest son. To the outside world the Duke often appeared a somewhat daunting figure, but he delighted in playing games with his children and taking them on expeditions on their ponies. There were theatricals

Constance, Duchess of Westminster, by John Everett Millais. She died in 1880 aged forty-five.

Katherine, Duchess of Westminster, *the Duke of Westminster's second wife. She was twenty-four when they married in 1882, and there was a thirty-two-year difference in their ages. She outlived her step-children and all but one of her own children, dying in 1941.*

*Spring Cottage,
a photograph taken by
Henry Taunt in 1875
showing George Devey's
addition to the original
cottage, which is hidden
by trees to the right.*

too, in the Christmas season, and the youngest daughter remembers her father and his son-in-law, the Marquess of Ormonde, bringing the house down as Babes in the Wood, dressed in children's frocks and socks.[14]

Two teenage guests during one summer were Winston Churchill and his brother Jack, who were given lessons in rowing and punting on the Thames by the Cliveden boatman, Ben Cooper. The boatman years later told David Astor how these two precocious boys took him into Maidenhead and gave him a meal and a cigar.

In 1893 the Duke of Westminster, with reluctance, sold Cliveden. It was not included in the settled estate, so he was able to dispose of it as he wished, and its sale enabled him to make better provision for his younger sons and daughters without having to curtail his evergrowing expenditure on charities. Another factor was that the rebuilding work at Eaton Hall had been finished, and this once again became their principal country house. However, parting with Cliveden was a sad moment for the family and drew an indignant response from Queen Victoria. She wrote to the Duke from Florence in April:

The Queen thanks the Duke of Westminster for his letter of Monday. She is deeply grieved to read its contents and laments the necessity the Duke feels himself under of selling dear beautiful Cliveden. The Duchess frequently told her she hoped he had given up the idea of selling. The Duke must excuse the Queen if she says she thinks he had built too much at Eaton and that if that had not been so, Cliveden might have been retained. He will miss it very much the Queen is sure and the Duchess and the children even more so. We grieve to think that we shall probably never see it again. The Queen is however glad he thinks that any rate the beauties and quiet of the place will be preserved, but it is grievous to think of its falling into these hands![15]

'These hands' was a reference to William Waldorf Astor, who took possession of Cliveden on 15 August 1893.

CHAPTER VIII

The Astors

CLIVEDEN 1893–1967

THE NEW OWNER OF CLIVEDEN, William Waldorf Astor, like the Duke of Sutherland and the Duke of Westminster before him, was immensely rich. His great-grandfather, John Jacob Astor, was from Waldorf in Germany, where the family was involved in two disparate activities, the making and selling of musical instruments and as butchers. In 1783, at the age of twenty-one, John Jacob left Europe on an immigrant ship with twenty-

five dollars and seven flutes in his luggage to join his brother in New York. His skills as a salesman and entrepreneur, and his energy, enabled him to build a fortune through the music business, then the fur trade and finally through real estate on the island of Manhattan. When he died in 1848 he was the richest man in America. John Jacob's son, William Backhouse Astor, who died in 1875, also in due course became the richest man in America and left his son John Jacob Astor III $200,000,000. When John Jacob died in 1890, his son William Waldorf Astor in his turn became America's richest citizen.[1]

William Waldorf Astor was a large man with bright blue eyes and a sweeping moustache, but his looks masked a shy and cantankerous nature. His early life was spartan, even though he lived in a household of unlimited grandeur, and he was educated at home. The family business did not attract him greatly, and in 1877 he ventured into the rough and tumble of American politics, for which he was ill suited. Vilified by the press in a way that scarred him for life, his thoughts turned to living abroad. The chance came in 1882, when the President of the United States, Chester

Right:
William Waldorf Astor, later 1st Viscount Astor (1848-1919), a painting by Hubert von Herkomer that hangs in the Terrace Dining Room. William Waldorf bought Cliveden in 1893 and immediately embarked on extensive alterations to the interior of the house. He gave Cliveden to his eldest son Waldorf on Waldorf's marriage to Nancy anghorne in 1906; they, in turn, gave it to the National Trust in 1942.

William Waldorf Astor and Mamie, with their children Waldorf (right), John Jacob (later 1st Baron Astor of Hever) and Pauline. Mamie died at the age of thirty-six. This made William Waldorf's shy and austere nature even more pronounced and created a somewhat intimidating atmosphere at Cliveden, in which his children were to grow up. Mamie's death put particular pressure on the fourteen-year-old Pauline, who was expected to take over as chatelaine.

Arthur, wishing to reward Astor for his support of the Republican party, offered him the post of United States Minister to Italy. His duties in Rome were minimal, and for three years he and his wife Mamie absorbed European culture and he indulged his passion for collecting Old Master paintings, armour and illuminated manuscripts. While in Italy he wrote the first of his two historical novels, *Valentino*, based on the life of Cesare Borgia.

William Waldorf's time in Italy ended with the arrival of a Democrat in the White House. He returned to America and after several uneasy years decided to turn his back on his homeland and the source of his vast wealth. In 1891 he brought his wife and three children, Waldorf, Pauline and John Jacob (who had all been threatened with kidnap), to England, announcing, it is said, that 'America is not a fit place for a gentleman to live'.[2] He rented Taplow Court and Lansdowne House in London and entered his sons for Eton.

WILLIAM WALDORF AND HIS PURCHASE OF CLIVEDEN

In 1893, two years after coming to England, William Waldorf bought Cliveden from the Duke of Westminster for $1.25 million (having rented it for the previous year). There was only one cloud on the horizon, which was the deterioration of his wife's health. Three days before Christmas 1894 Mamie died at the age of thirty-six. The introspective side of William Waldorf's nature soon became more pronounced, and he grew more eccentric and austere. He threw himself into building projects at Cliveden and in London. Mamie's death put considerable strain on Pauline who, aged fourteen, was expected to take over as chatelaine of Cliveden. Michael Astor in his book *Tribal Feeling* explained that William Waldorf's

> *...weekend parties in the country, planned many months in advance, lacked that sense of joie de vivre which the word 'party' is supposed to suggest. Guests were told exactly when to arrive; and when they arrived they were greeted by a secretary (or by his daughter...) who showed them to their rooms and told them where, and at what time, they would assemble before meals. The rest of the weekend was according to a schedule, short periods set aside for walking, driving, resting, eating, and finally sleep.*[3]

On one occasion a guest at Cliveden finished writing letters earlier than she anticipated and went for a stroll in the garden. A servant hastily explained that Mr Astor expected people to follow the schedules that had been settled upon. She demanded her carriage with the intention of leaving immediately, only to be told that Mr Astor did not allow a carriage to be called at a time that had not been agreed.[4]

William Waldorf, when dealing with those he employed, issued instructions and did not tolerate any discussion about his decisions, and his social equals fared little better. His bad manners and inflexibility led to several well-publicized rows. One of these related to a section of a redwood tree, mounted on a stand, that he brought to Cliveden from California in 1897. The *Daily Mail* published an article under the title 'A Millionaire's Wager', reporting that Mr Astor had wagered £500 with General Owen Williams that he could dine twenty-seven people round the section of tree, which was 16 feet in diameter. The article continued with an account of the dinner and the supposed guest list. William Waldorf was furious, feeling that this fictitious story portrayed him in a frivolous light, and he sued the *Daily Mail* for libel.[5]

An Eccentric at Cliveden

Another instance of his eccentric behaviour related to the Westminsters' Visitors Book. After his purchase of Cliveden, he received a letter from the Duke of Westminster requesting the return of the Visitors Book, which had been left by mistake. William Waldorf refused on the grounds that anything that remained in the house legally belonged to him. The dispute ran for years, and it was not until the next generation that the book was returned to its rightful owner.

The Royal Family was treated no differently. William Waldorf showed scant respect for the Prince of Wales and his set, and criticized them openly. Yet, at the same time, he craved public recognition and acceptance.

Cliveden was a like a court, with governesses, tutors, secretaries, servants and attendants ruled over by a lonely autocrat. His flag was raised at 9.00 a.m. and lowered at sunset. In this sombre atmosphere his sons Waldorf and John Jacob and his daughter Pauline were brought up. He gave the boys the opportunity to develop as English gentlemen, and they went to Eton and Oxford. When the family was alone at Cliveden, Pauline read aloud at mealtimes from one of his favourite books about European history. He listened while consuming elaborate dishes selected by him a week in advance from an array of cookery books and beautifully prepared by the chef.

In 1899 William Waldorf became a British citizen. The American press described him as 'the richest man that America ever owned and that disowned America'.[6] In a country where money was God, he was viewed as a traitor. It was perhaps this that made him feel vulnerable to assassination, and in later years he slept with two revolvers beside his bed.

Alterations to the interior of Cliveden began shortly after William Waldorf bought the house, and practically nothing survives of Charles Barry's interiors. His architect was John Loughborough Pearson, known principally for his church

Right:
The Staircase, leading from the Great Hall, with newel posts carved by W. S. Frith. The lower figures represent the seventeenth-century Duke of Buckingham and his mistress Anna Maria, Countess of Shrewsbury; the upper figures represent William and Isabella de Turville, twelfth-century owners of the Cliveden estate. The Staircase formed part of William Waldorf's remodelling of the interior.

The French Dining Room. The room came from the Château d'Asnières, near Paris, and dates from the mid-eighteenth century. It was bought by William Waldorf in 1897 and replaced Charles Barry's Dining Room shown on page 109.

architecture. He had built the remarkable Astor town house and office at 2 Temple Place on the Embankment in 1895 and used a number of the craftsmen and ideas from that commission at Cliveden. Pearson was in his seventies and gave much of the responsibility for carrying out the work to his son, Frank. Frank oversaw the carved interiors, executed in a variety of period styles, both at 2 Temple Place and at Cliveden. Some of the rooms in mid-seventeenth-century style were specifically designed as the setting for his large collections of sculpture, tapestries and furniture.

Pearson greatly enlarged the Hall by opening arches through to what had been the Morning Room on the left and the Staircase on the right, and panelled it in oak, adding Corinthian columns and pilasters. He bought in Paris three tapestries for the Hall from the series of *Arts of War*, not knowing at the time that they had once belonged to Lord Orkney and had hung at Cliveden until the fire of 1795.

The Staircase, designed by the Pearsons, has figures on each newel post, which were carved by W. S. Frith to represent people associated with the history of Cliveden. The idea no doubt came from such houses as Hatfield and Blickling, and had already been used at 2 Temple Place.

William Waldorf commissioned a painting of the *Banquet of the Gods* from an artist brought from Italy for the ceiling of Barry's Dining Room. However, this was subsequently replaced. On 27 January 1897, when William Waldorf and his daughter were staying in Paris, she noted:

Papa went out with Allard [his French decorator] to look at several things and among them a chatelet built by the King for Mme de Pompadour – the

An eighteenth-century marble statue in the Long Garden, bought by William Waldorf in Venice in 1894 as a figure of Doge Morosini, perhaps in the guise of Marco Polo.

banquet hall it seems is very beautiful and almost the same size as our dining room at Cliveden.[7]

The room they saw was from the Château d'Asnières near Paris, designed by Nicolas Pineau in 1750. Louis XV leased the château after the owner's death in 1757 and lent it to Madame de Pompadour. The exactly matching size of the room and its historical associations led to the purchase and installation of the room at Cliveden, in what has become known as the French Dining Room. The Rococo *boiseries* are equal in quality to the finest surviving in France.

Additions were also made by William Waldorf to the gardens. He created the Long Garden with its topiary and eighteenth-century statuary, an expression of his love of Italy. He extended the Water Garden and bought the Pagoda made for the Paris Exhibition of 1867 from the sale of Bagatelle, Lord Hertford's villa in Paris, in 1900. Perhaps his most important acquisition for Cliveden was the famous Balustrade from the gardens of the Villa Borghese in Rome, set up in September and October 1896 on the Parterre, parallel with Winde's terrace. It was carved by Giuseppe di Giacomo and Paolo Massini

The Long Garden, created by William Waldorf, where much of his important collection of statuary is displayed. The eighteenth-century north Italian figures in the foreground represent characters from the Commedia dell'Arte.

The Borghese
Balustrade, *a watercolour*
by John Singer Sargent.
The seventeenth-century
Balustrade was bought by
William Waldorf in 1896
from the Villa Borghese in
Rome and positioned on
the Parterre. It was one of
his most notable
purchases.

for Cardinal Scipione Borghese in 1618-19. As reconstructed, lengths of stone balustrading alternate with sections of red brick wall with stone seats, and at the corners and ends there are pedestals for statues carved with the eagles and dragons of the house of Borghese. The Italian Government attempted to prevent the removal of the Balustrade, but it was decided in a court of law that, being purely decorative, it could not be classified as a work of art; however, the antique statues that were originally placed upon it were considered to be works of art, and their removal was prohibited.

Other important items in William Waldorf's collection were the Roman sarcophagi, which he positioned against the great yew hedges on the north side of the forecourt. As well as the sarcophagi, Roman and Italian statues were placed throughout the grounds.

A fluted Roman sarcophagus of c. AD 150-200, with at either end lions accompanied by their keepers. The lions are tearing to pieces humped cattle, the first-known appearance of this species of animal on a Roman sarcophagus.

The Endymion sarcophagus. Roman in origin, and dating from AD c. 230, it came from the Villa Borghese in Rome.

The large shell fountain, the *Fountain of Love,* at the north end of the drive, was made for William Waldorf by Thomas Waldo Story (son of Wetmore Story), an American sculptor living in Rome. The fountain was sculpted in 1897 and replaced the statue of the Duke of Sutherland, which William Waldorf moved to its present site beyond the Parterre.

William Waldorf did not like the thought of his neighbours walking through the grounds and so built a wall around part of the estate that was surmounted

by jagged bits of glass. Thereafter, he was referred to locally as 'walled-off' Astor. His love of Cliveden is not in doubt, and he left an account of his feelings for the place through a series of short stories.

PUBLISHER AND STORY-WRITER

In 1892 William Wardorf had bought the Liberal newspaper the *Pall Mall Gazette* and turned it into a Conservative paper that echoed his views. He had literary aspirations of his own, and Harry Cust, the Tory Member of Parliament whom William Waldorf appointed editor, had difficulty diverting William Waldorf's offerings but succeeded on the grounds that his efforts were more suitable for a 'literary' magazine. William Waldorf promptly founded a monthly, called the *Pall Mall Magazine,* which concentrated on the romantic and the antiquarian and where his short stories could be printed. Some of these were published in book form as *Pharaoh's Daughter and Other Stories.* Several were written as if by a fictitious seventeenth-century character named Andrew Deepgrove. Through Deepgrove, William Waldorf expressed his own feelings about Cliveden in what he supposed to be an earlier literary style. In 'Cliveden Lights and Shades', he wrote:

> *Cliefden alone, rarer than the suttlest imagining, grows day by day more incomparable. Most beautiful of all is it in November, at the fall of the leaf, when, walking through the hedgerows upon fallen fragrant leaves, with the tree-tops thinning overhead, I pause to watch the leaf that from the topmost bough falls flickering.*[8]

Deepgrove looks back nostalgically in 'The Romance of Cliveden':

> *It is now thirty-four yeares since I first trod the greensward of Cliefden,... The first time that ever I looked from yonder Terrace upon the glistening Thames, and marked its course*

Fountain of Love
*by Thomas Waldo Story,
carved in marble and
volcanic rock in Rome and
dated 1897.*

Wounded Amazon,
*carved in marble by
William Waldorf Astor,
signed and dated 1870.
This is the only known
sculpture by William
Waldorf. He was taught in
Rome by William
Wetmore Story (father of
Thomas Waldo Story),
and this figure was
probably carved under
Story's supervision.*

between the lofty Cliff on this side, and the broad Meadows on that, till its silver thread passes from sight miles away beneath Maydenhead Bridge, it seemed to me that never could the Eye of Man have rested upon a scene of more exquisite enchantment.[9]

In 1903 his daughter Pauline married Captain Herbert Spender-Clay, and he was left without a hostess. It was at this time that he bought the medieval castle of Hever in Kent. Hever, even more than Cliveden, appealed to his sense of history. It was here that Anne Boleyn had lived before her marriage to Henry VIII, and her unhappy spirit was thought still to wander the castle. At Hever, William Waldorf built a 'Tudor village', where he housed his visitors. At night he pulled up the drawbridge and secluded himself and his guests from the world outside. By 1910 he had spent the staggering sum of £10 million on Hever.

Rape of Proserpina, *a bronze group of the sixteenth century attributed to Vincenzo de' Rossi. This was one of William Waldorf's finest acquisitions.*

Cliveden was not to remain as Willam Waldorf had planned it for long. His son, the young Waldorf Astor, may have inherited some of his father's shyness but he did not inherit his political views. He was liberal in spirit and a reformist with a 'social conscience', who wanted to 'get things done'. At Eton he held the most coveted positions in the school. He also excelled at Oxford, where he strained his heart rowing. This led to his health being a cause for concern for the rest of his life.

THE ARRIVAL OF NANCY

On a transatlantic crossing in December 1905 Waldorf met and fell in love with Nancy Langhorne, and in the following March they became engaged. Nancy was not the chaste English aristocrat that William Waldorf was hoping for but a twenty-six year-old Virginian divorcee with a six-year-old son, Bobbie Shaw. She was one of the five beautiful Langhorne sisters, the eldest of whom married the artist Charles Dana Gibson and became the model for American beauty through his creation of 'The Gibson Girl'.

William Waldorf trusted his son's judgment and said to Nancy, 'If you are good enough for Waldorf, then you will be good for me'.[10] These words were supported with the gift to Waldorf of Cliveden and to Nancy a magnificent tiara containing the famous Sancy diamond (now in the Louvre). The 55-carat

Left: Nancy Langhorne, later Viscountess Astor (1879–1964), *by John Singer Sargent. This portrait of 1908 was one of the last of Sargent's society portraits. His first intention was to paint her carrying her year-old son Bill on her back, which explains her stance in the portrait. From the time of her marriage to Waldorf in 1906 she became a famous hostess, and she and her husband entertained politicians from all political parties from both sides of the Atlantic; famous writers; diplomats; and actors. She is best known as the first woman Member of Parliament to take her seat in the House of Commons. This was in 1919. The portrait hangs today in the Great Hall at Cliveden.*

diamond had belonged to James I and Charles I, and was later worn by Louis XV at his coronation, and this clearly appealed to the romantic side of William Waldorf's character. Waldorf and Nancy were married quietly in London on 3 May 1906. The date and place, All Souls, Langham Place, were kept secret from the press. The Church of England ban on the marriage of divorced persons was waived.

The bride and groom made Cliveden their principal home and Nancy, who had been told by her father-in-law that he would never return, had no inhibitions about transforming the house:

the keynote of the place when I took over was splendid gloom. Tapestries and ancient leather furniture filled most of the rooms. The place looked better when I had put in books and chintz curtains and covers, and flowers.[11]

Nancy Astor, wearing the tiara containing the 55-carat Sancy diamond. The tiara was given to Nancy by William Waldorf on her marriage to his son Waldorf in 1906.

She ordered the stone antiquities to be removed from the Hall and had the entire Minton tiled floor replaced by stone flags.

When in 1907 Nancy's first son, William Waldorf (always known as Bill), was born, his grandfather was so delighted that he forgot his vow and sent a message that he was coming to Cliveden to see him. Nancy took to her bed in horror. On arrival he surveyed the changes at first without comment and then said to his son, 'The first joy of possession is to change everything around and remould it nearer to the heart's desire'.[12] Nancy, on being told of his reaction, decided that she would receive her father-in-law in her bedroom. He was charm personified and was delighted with his grandson.

As soon as Nancy moved into Cliveden she became a figure of great interest. Only

The Drawing Room in William Waldorf's time, after alterations had been made to the Westminsters' scheme of decoration (see page 122).

*The English-born
Princess, later Queen,
Marie of Romania
photographed at Cliveden.
She met Waldorf in 1902
and later described this as
'the starting point of a
very dear friendship'.
Waldorf and his sister
Pauline became close
friends with the Princess
and stayed with her in
Romania on several
occasions, while the
Princess was a frequent
guest at Cliveden. On the
left is a framed photograph
of Nancy.*

just over five feet in height, she was both beautiful and amusing, with brilliant blue eyes brimming with vitality. Edward VII was eager to meet her, and arrangements were made for a visit. The royal guest found everything 'so agreeable' that he did not leave until eight o'clock in the evening. On a later occasion the King wished to play bridge; Nancy declined, fortunately to the King's amusement, with the now famous phrase, 'I am afraid I can't tell a King from a Knave'.[13]

Another royal visitor to Cliveden was the English-born Princess (later Queen) Marie of Romania. She came to England in 1902 to attend Edward VII's coronation and it was then that she met the young Waldorf, a meeting

143

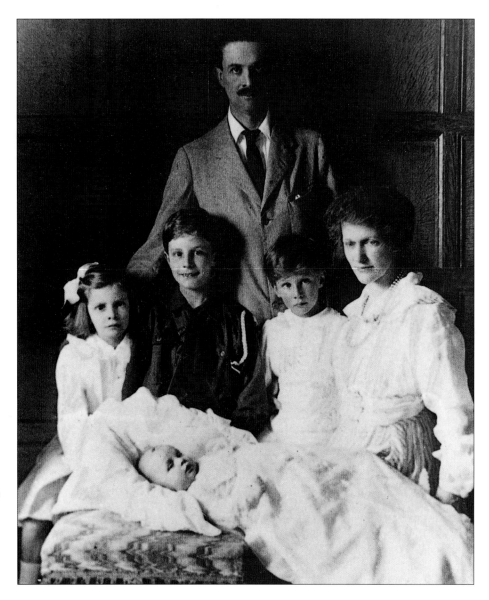

Waldorf and Nancy Astor, with their children Bill, Wissie, David and Michael, a photograph taken in 1916. Their last child, Jakie, was born two years later.

she described as 'the starting point of a very dear friendship which has meant much in my life'.[14] Waldorf and his sister Pauline became very close friends with the Princess and paid several visits to Romania. The butler at Cliveden, Edwin Lee, described the extreme formality of Queen Marie's entourage:

When she came to Cliveden she was always accompanied by an equerry, who had the rank of Baron and was a very tall man. In the morning he used to station himself in full uniform at the foot of the staircase leading down to the hall and wait for her to descend, standing stiffly to attention sometimes for as much as an hour. As soon as he saw her on the stairs, he bowed very low and, as her feet touched the floor, advanced and ceremoniously kissed her hand.[15]

Waldorf was determined to make amends for what he saw as his father's lack of public service. He stood and was elected Member of Parliament for Plymouth in 1910, taking up a position on the left of the Conservative Party.

He used Cliveden and 4 St James's Square in London to bring together people who would help him pursue his particular interests, which included agriculture, Anglo-American relations and health. (Directly as a result of his efforts the Ministry of Health was created in 1919, with Waldorf as the first Ministerial Parliamentary Private Secretary.) Many of his guests were friends from Oxford days, who became the 'Round Table' group. They included Philip Kerr (who became 11th Marquess of Lothian in 1930), Geoffrey Dawson (later editor of *The Times* when owned by Waldorf's brother John) and Robert Brand (who later married Nancy's sister Phyllis). They all played an important part in the lives of Waldorf and Nancy.

In 1911 Waldorf persuaded his father to buy *The Observer* newspaper, then edited by James Garvin. Three years later Waldorf himself took over *The Observer,* and so began perhaps the longest and most remarkable relationship between proprietor and editor in the history of English newspapers.

CLIVEDEN IN THE FIRST WORLD WAR

When war broke out in 1914, Waldorf volunteered for the army but failed the medical. He disliked the thought of being in England when his friends were in the trenches and insisted on 'a disagreeable job'. He became a supervisor of training camps for Southern Command. At the beginning of the war Waldorf offered Cliveden as a hospital to the British Army, but it was decided that the house would be too difficult to adapt. Undaunted, he offered it to the Canadians, who accepted it and created a hospital in the covered tennis court and the bowling alley. Several other buildings on the estate were occupied by staff.

By 1915 The Duchess of Connaught Red Cross Hospital (named for the wife of the Governor General of Canada) could accommodate 110 patients, and it apparently ended up by taking 600. The first ministerial visit to the hospital was made on 3 May 1915 by the First Lord of the Admiralty, Winston Churchill, and on 20 July of that year the King and Queen paid an official visit.

Nancy worked with great vigour, and her personality worked wonders on the patients. Stories abounded about how she willed men to live – such as

The Duchess of Connaught Red Cross Hospital for Canadian servicemen at Cliveden, photographed during the First World War. Nancy spent much time in the hospital with the wounded and had a legendary ability to instil in them the will to live.

The Astors' covered tennis court was converted for hospital use. Nancy was playing tennis on the covered court when news was brought of the outbreak of the First World War.

the two sailors who had come in to Plymouth after the Battle of Jutland. They were badly wounded, and they had turned their faces to the wall and given up hope. Nancy asked where they came from and, on learning from one that he came from Yorkshire, she retorted, 'No wonder you don't want to live, if you come from Yorkshire!' The man raised himself on an elbow and said, 'Repeat that!' Yorkshire, he pointed out, was the finest place in the world and if anyone said otherwise it meant they knew nothing about it. 'To hell with the Battle of Jutland, I am going back to Yorkshire.' He did.[16]

The hospital was very effective, and of the twenty-four thousand who were treated there only forty servicemen and two nurses died. They were buried in the Canadian Cemetery at Cliveden, a place of haunting beauty dominated by a symbolic figure representing Canada. In February 1917 the Australian Bertram MacKennal had sculpted a head of Nancy, and later that year she asked him to design and execute a figure to stand in the Cemetery. Nancy herself was clearly the inspiration for the face of the figure. The inscription runs:

THEY ARE AT PEACE. GOD PROVED THEM AND
FOUND THEM WORTHY FOR HIMSELF.

From 1914 until 1918 Cliveden was run on wartime economy lines, with sheep and poultry on the lawns and potatoes and cabbages in place of

146

flowers. Willie Bridgeman wrote to his wife on 11 December 1915, 'The food was not war-fare, but was limited in quantity, and we had no alcohol – and only women servants!'[17] The men were of course in the trenches.

During the war Waldorf's political ambitions began to take precedence over his military life and, helped by strong editorials in *The Observer*, he played a part in removing the Asquith coalition government. He was an active supporter of Lloyd George and his policies, and from 1915 to 1918 he was his Parliamentary Private Secretary, and acted as the Prime Minister's eyes and ears in the House of Commons. Other members of the Round Table such as Philip Kerr were also included in the Lloyd George administration.

WILLIAM WALDORF'S ELEVATION TO THE PEERAGE

Waldorf's important position at the very centre of political life was threatened by an event that took place in January 1916: the conferring of a barony on his

Top: The Canadian Cemetery at Cliveden, where those who died in the hospital are buried. Above: A detail of Bertram MacKennal's symbolic figure of Canada in the memorial garden.

father at the suggestion of Lloyd George's rival Asquith. It was the recognition William Waldorf had wished for, and his enormous gifts and benefactions to the Red Cross and numerous other organizations before and during the war made it seem particularly well deserved in the context of the time.

Waldorf and Nancy were not consulted and were furious. Waldorf's very promising career in the House of Commons would end on William Waldorf's death as he would have to take his father's seat in the House of Lords. William Waldorf was appalled by his son's reaction to the honour and announced that he never wanted to see him again – and he never did. He also altered his will to divert money from his son to his grandchildren.

The 1st Lord Astor appeared only twice in the Lords, once in 1916, when he took his seat, and again in 1917 after he received a viscountcy. The coat of arms he had designed for himself featured a falcon. This was the falcon that appeared on the shield of the Astorga family in the Middle Ages in Spain. From a young age he had been obsessed with his family's genealogy and wished to show it in an aristocratic light, which gave encouragement to the myth that the Astors were descended from Spanish noblemen.

William Waldorf was closest to his second son, John, who sent him regular letters from the Front that genuinely moved him. John was wounded twice and on the second occasion lost a leg. The old man decided, for the second

The visit of King George V and Queen Mary to the Canadian hospital on 20 July 1915. At this time the hospital could accommodate 110 patients, and by the end of the war the number had risen to 600.

The dome of the Octagon Temple. William Waldorf commissioned Frank Loughborough Pearson to remodel the interior of Leoni's building of the eighteenth century. He converted it into a family chapel by removing the floor supporting the upper and lower rooms and creating a single cruciform space. The colourful mosaics are sixteen designs by Clayton & Bell. This shows Our Lord and the Blessed Virgin Enthroned and the archangels.

time in his life, on the extraordinarily generous act of moving out of the house he was living in and giving it to one of his sons.

William Waldorf spent his last, solitary days in a Regency house in Brighton, eating superb food and drinking fine wine. One of the few people he saw was his eldest grandson, Bill Astor. Whenever Bill came to stay, he did his best to wean him away from Nancy's teetotalism and her advocacy of the merits of Christian Science.

William Waldorf died on 18 October 1919 at the age of seventy-one, and his ashes were placed in the Octagon Temple at Cliveden. He had made no intimate friends, and his shyness, lack of tact and awkwardness, and his inability to communicate with people, had made him lonely and embittered. Waldorf felt the blow strongly and, having not seen his father for four years, was not expecting the end so soon. Waldorf's parliamentary seat, the Southern Division of Plymouth, was automatically vacated, and he took up his seat in the House of Lords as the 2nd Viscount Astor. He held radical views about the Upper House, and on two occasions attempted to introduce legislation to do away with the hereditary principle and introduce life peerages for both men and women.

NANCY IN POLITICS

Female suffrage (for women over 30) had become law in February 1918 and for the first time a woman could now stand for parliament. After William Waldorf died and Waldorf had become the 2nd Viscount Astor, there was press speculation as to whether Nancy would take over her husband's constituency. Nancy was not keen on the idea but agreed to stand in order to give Waldorf time to organize the introduction of legislation that would make it possible for him to renounce his peerage and thus sit again in the Commons for his Plymouth constituency. (The law permitting this was not introduced until 1963.) Waldorf, with his undoubted and proven talents, could have had a ministerial career in the House of Lords, and it is surprising that he did not do so, but it was his feelings for Nancy that dictated the course of his career. He was so enamoured of his wife, and so admiring of her talents, that he never regretted making way for her. He virtually became her political manager, devoting most of his time and attention to her needs. In spite of his self-effacing nature, he remained the ultimate boss in her eyes, although she became increasingly wilful and difficult with age.

Nancy was elected by a majority of 5,203 votes on 28 November 1919 in a fanfare of world publicity and came to Cliveden the following day. When the

The interior of the Octagon Temple, remodelled and consecrated in 1906. The triptych, altar cross and furniture are by Barkentin & Krall. The chapel contains the ashes of the 1st, 2nd and 3rd Viscount Astor.

couple arrived at the *Fountain of Love* in front of the house, the estate workers were waiting with a Victorian carriage. Nancy and Waldorf were pulled slowly up to the house by the cheering workers, past the bonfires lit for the occasion.

Nancy's reception in the House of Commons was not so enthusiastic as the six hundred or so men disliked the idea of the arrival of a woman in their midst. Even her own relations who were Members of Parliament found it hard to speak to her inside the Palace of Westminster. Nancy's courage in coping with this situation was remarkable. She spoke of her experience with Churchill in a BBC radio broadcast on 9 November 1937:

Winston Churchill, who I knew quite well, like many other members of the House, who I knew intimately, simply could not bring themselves to speak to me once I was in the House. After about two years I met Winston at dinner and he congratulated me on my performance. I asked him why he

had not spoken to me before and he replied, 'We thought if we could freeze
you out, we would get rid of the lot'. I asked him, 'Why did you want to
get rid of the lot?' 'Well,' replied Winston, 'when you entered the House of
Commons I felt as though some woman had entered my bath and I had
nothing to protect myself with except my sponge.'

Winston and Nancy never really recognized each other's qualities and on one
famous occasion at breakfast, when Nancy became exasperated by him, she
proclaimed, 'Winston, if I was married to you I'd put poison in your coffee.'
To this he replied, 'Nancy, if I was married to you, I'd drink it.'[18]

Barry's classical villa at Cliveden and his Gothic palace at Westminster
became equally important in Nancy's life. She came to need them both;
neither would have been anything like as useful to her or to the causes she
took up without the other. Unlike Waldorf, she loved being the centre of
attention, and Cliveden's position made it the perfect stage for her. After the
war the servants returned and the corridors resounded to the noise of her five
children and an assortment of dogs. Walter Elliot, who entered the Commons
at about the same time as Nancy, caught the atmosphere of Cliveden:

Tea on the terrace of
the Pavilion on the west
side of the house
in about 1907.

*Weekend parties might contain people of high society, people of no
society... I don't know which was more pleasant, to appear at tea-time in
winter when the tea was set in the centre hall before the big fire, or in
summer, when it was laid out with infinite details, under a pavilion roof at
the end of the broad terrace. Tea, did I say? It was more like a Bedouin
encampment. There was a table for tea, a table for cakes, a table for children,
a table for grown-ups, a table for more grown-ups and generally a nomadic
group coming and going somewhere in the neighbourhood of Nancy herself.
Cushions, papers, people were mixed in a noble disarray. Nancy presided
over the whole affair like a blend between Juno at the siege of Troy, and one
of the leading Valkyries caracoling over an appropriate battlefield.*[19]

Waldorf and Nancy were compulsive entertainers, and the diversity of the
guests was extraordinary. Members of the Round Table, now in positions of
influence, were frequent guests as were other policy makers, including
delegates of the League of Nations. The Astors were both conspicuous and
glamorous, and they attracted celebrities from all walks of life. Publicity
followed their every pronouncement and every party. When they travelled

153

abroad they were treated like royalty, particularly in America, where they were seen as unofficial ambassadors from Britain.

Nancy's speeches (often written by her husband) concentrated on social causes. She railed against the wickedness of alcohol and hated the drink lobby, referring to some members in the Lords as 'the Beerage'. In 1923 she introduced a Private Member's Bill to limit the sale of alcohol to those over eighteen years of age.

Waldorf used his newspaper *The Observer* and the House of Lords to further his causes, one of them being agriculture, and he co-authored three books on the subject. In one, the authors explored the radical concept of the benefits of public ownership of land. Waldorf's brother John, too, became a newspaper proprietor when in 1922 he bought *The Times.* John joined Nancy in the House of Commons, and the two families had friends in common who were visitors at both Cliveden and Hever.

FRIENDSHIPS AND GUESTS

The Cliveden Visitors Book is a 'Who's Who' of the period. The most famous name from the world of theatre, George Bernard Shaw, first stayed in 1926,

Waldorf and Nancy invited distinguished people from all walks of life to Cliveden. Here they are photographed in 1932 with President Roosevelt (second from right) and his wife, and their eldest son (right).

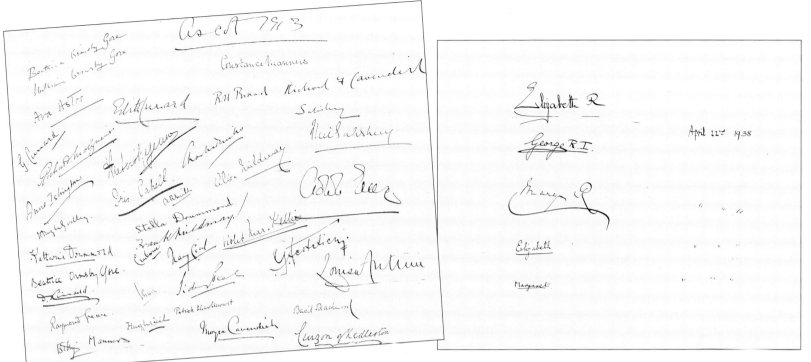

The Cliveden Visitors Book is a 'Who's Who' of the period. The page above has the signatures of the party for Ascot in 1913 that included Lord Curzon of Kedleston and members of the Manners, Cavendish and Cecil families.

The visit of the King and Queen, accompanied by Queen Mary and the Princesses Margaret and Elizabeth in 1938. Royal visits to Cliveden have taken place throughout its history.

and his signature, and that of his wife Charlotte, appears frequently from 1927 onwards. G. B. S. and Nancy could hardly have been further apart in their attitudes. Winston Churchill described them as they left London for a highly publicized visit to the Soviet Union in 1931 as 'the World's most famous intellectual Clown and Pantaloon in one, and the charming Columbine of the capitalist pantomime'.[20]

Shaw was in his seventies and at the height of his fame, and Nancy was a celebrity of almost equal renown within the English-speaking world. Shaw himself was certainly aware of the improbability of the friendship and referring to his wife in a letter to Nancy wrote, 'She is fond of you. So am I. I don't know why.'[21]

While staying at Cliveden during the severe winter of 1928 Shaw was putting the finishing touches to his last great play, *The Apple Cart*. It was his custom to hold reading parties for distinguished actors and friends, and *The Apple Cart* was given its first airing at Cliveden between Christmas and New Year. Charlotte Shaw wrote to Blanche Patch, Shaw's secretary:

Mr Shaw read the play, (all we had of it) to the party here and had an immense success. All that political part went splendidly: better than the love scene! They were wild to hear the last Act which he had just finished. Have you any of it typed?[22]

*The playwright George
Bernard Shaw (right) was
a frequent visitor to
Cliveden. Next to him
stands Nancy Astor and
to her right Charlie
Chaplin and the aviatrix
Amy Johnson.*

Shaw urged his secretary to send
him the last act immediately as
he was keen to get back to London but could not do so until he
had satisfied his Cliveden audi-
ence. Clearly the readings were
much enjoyed, although some
guests were surprised that Shaw
laughed more heartily than anyone else at the jokes. The playwright's attachment to Nancy
continued for the rest of his life and in 1950, when he lay dying, she was
almost the only friend he wanted by his side.

Friendship with the Shaws intensified another friendship, that with T. E.
Lawrence. The Shaws and Lawrence were close friends and, when Colonel
Lawrence took the name of Aircraftsman Shaw in 1927 (in a vain attempt at
anonymity), there were those who came to the conclusion that the Shaws and

*The Cliveden Visitors
Book for Christmas 1927
showing George Bernard
Shaw's signature.*

he were kinsfolk. Nancy and Lawrence's association had begun after she wrote to him in 1924, 'I am one of the people who are very wealthy and would like a copy of your book, but I don't promise to read it.'[23] Nancy had a taste for mixing with the famous, and if she made up her mind that she wanted someone to be a friend and frequent visitor she nearly always got her way. But her friendship with Lawrence had a different quality. He was deeply depressed and found her understanding, as he showed in his letters. On one occasion, when returning late to his quarters, 'Aircraftsman Shaw' was stopped and asked for an explanation. He gave as his excuse that he had been detained at dinner with Lord and Lady Astor and George Bernard Shaw. His fellow airmen laughed.

A drawing by Augustus John of T. E. Lawrence, who corresponded with Nancy and was another of Cliveden's regular visitors.

Although Waldorf persuaded Nancy to give up hunting when she had children, she craved that excitement and persuaded Lawrence to take her riding on his motorbike at high speed. Waldorf remonstrated, 'Really, Lawrence, my wife should not be encouraged to find new ways of breaking her neck!'[24] It was, ironically, Lawrence who broke his neck falling off a motorbike. The tragic news was given to Nancy during a lunch party at Cliveden.

Nancy described her technique for dealing with most of her guests (which was very similar to Sir George Warrender's arrangements a hundred years earlier):

> *There was lots to do at Cliveden. My guests would go off and amuse themselves or talk to people they wanted to, or read, ride, walk, explore the grounds or play tennis. My rule was not to appear before lunch. I never interfered with them. That was how I got clever people like Arthur James Balfour to stay.*[25]

Michael Astor in *Tribal Feeling* gave a vivid account of the quality of the verbal exchanges at Cliveden:

> *Were there ever such talkers brought together in one place? Bernard Shaw commanded an audience and his talk demanded one. But J. L. Garvin, Walter Elliot, Lionel Curtis and Geoffrey Dawson had to compete. Garvin would go ten minutes without eating when he was talking, otherwise he lost his place. Lionel Curtis on Federated Europe evoked a sense of timelessness, of something inexorable which had to be stated and had to be heard, impervious to Bobbie's aside, voicing our unspoken thoughts of 'Can't anyone tell him to shut up?' which carried to the end of the table and roused my mother to ask Bobbie to shut up, and through the various requests of 'shut up' Lionel boomed on, noble and unbowed.*[26]

Pages from Joyce Grenfell's photograph album of a weekend at Cliveden in the summer of 1929. Joyce Phipps, as she was born, was Nancy Astor's niece, and she spent much time at Cliveden both as a child and after her marriage to Reginald Grenfell. There were about thirty guests that weekend, among them David Bowes-Lyon (Queen Elizabeth's brother) and his wife Rachel, who was Waldorf Astor's niece, and the journalist and wit A. P. Herbert. Entertainments included tennis in the Forecourt, punting and swimming in the Thames.

MR LEE: THE BUTLER

The guests at Cliveden were famous, but so were the staff who looked after them. The structure and hierarchy were very precise in those days. The master of the household was the butler, Edwin Lee, who came to Cliveden in 1912 and remained until 1960. Although Nancy was difficult and demanding, her senior staff remained with her for decades. She kept their loyalty by treating them as people. On one occasion, when Lee could not stand Nancy's wilfulness any longer, he gave notice, announcing that he would be leaving at the end of the month. Nancy retorted, 'In that case, Lee, tell me where you're going because I'm coming with you'. Lee knew that he had lost and could not leave.[27]

Lee's description of life just before the First World War tells much about life at Cliveden and at 4 St James's Square:

Dinners between 50 and 60 were very frequent and probably two or three

balls for anything up to 500 or 600 would be given during the season... A fairly large staff was kept in both London and Cliveden but most of us used to travel between London and Cliveden. At that particular time we had a very fine French chef who was considered one of the best in the country and a very nice man to work with. He had five girls working with him. We also had a stillroom where all the bread and cake were made. Baking was done at Cliveden twice a week. The Head Stillroom Maid used to travel between London and Cliveden. One Under Stillroom Maid was kept in either place. There was a very large staff of gardeners and stablemen kept at Cliveden between 40 and 50 gardeners and about 10 or 12 stablemen. All the lawns on the pleasure grounds were mowed by horses with leather boots strapped over their iron shoes. In the house at Cliveden there was a housekeeper, 6 housemaids, 6 laundry maids and always one or two left in the kitchen apart from the travelling staff, also an

Odd Man who used to look after the boilers, carry coal, answer the telephone – a most useful man in every way.[28]

It was Lee who greeted the guests on arrival. In the Hall there was a list of who was staying and where they were sleeping. New arrivals were 'checked in' and were shown to their rooms in the same way as they are today, now that Cliveden is a hotel. Indeed, when the Earl of Stockton (formerly Harold Macmillan, who had been a frequent guest in the thirties) was asked what he thought of Cliveden becoming a hotel, he replied, 'but my dear boy, it always has been'.[29] Once guests had been shown to their rooms they had to fend for themselves, which was quite disconcerting for someone who had not stayed at Cliveden before. In due course they would run into Nancy or Waldorf and be warmly welcomed, but quite possibly not introduced to other members of the party.

Cliveden was (and still is) a labour-intensive house to look after. Guests' bedrooms then were without washbasins or running water, there was no lift and the fires in the thirty bedrooms and reception rooms had to be made up each day, so it was 'upstairs, downstairs' with a vengeance, with a hundred tons of coal each year being burned in the bedrooms.

Nancy ran the house in collusion with the butler. Lee's control over the Astor dinner parties was expert. He knew better than anyone who got on well with whom and would suggest alterations to the table plan. Nancy was always keen to cram as many people in as possible, which gave very little room for manoeuvre for either the guests or the footmen, and on one occasion Winston Churchill refused to eat anything: '30 dishes served and no damn room to eat one', he exclaimed. Nancy remarked later to Lee that it was perfectly all right because Mr Churchill could afford to lose a little weight. It was only when Lee discovered the more generous space given to each guest at Buckingham Palace that he won this battle with Nancy.

Lee enjoyed royal visits partly because he knew it was only then that Nancy was likely to be on time – Queen Mary was the only woman Nancy feared. On important occasions Nancy's maid, Rose Harrison, would put the clocks and watches on a few minutes to ensure that she was ready. Lee had an arrangement with Windsor Castle that they would telephone him as the royal visitor left.

BEHIND THE GREEN BAIZE DOOR

The main mansion and East Wing were for the family and guests, and the West Wing and beyond were part of a different world, entered through the

The stone chimneypiece in the Great Hall was bought by William Waldorf at the Spitzer sale in Paris in 1892. It dates from c. 1525 and probably came from the château of Arnay-le-Duc in Burgundy. The centre panel is of St George and the Dragon.

green baize door. The servants' quarters occupied over half the area of the house, and the servants outnumbered the family by more than three to one. The basement under the main house contained the butler's pantry, silver board, wine cellar and footmen's rooms. This male domain was linked by an underground corridor with the lower part of the West Wing and the Servants' Hall. Much of the ground floor of the West Wing was the housekeeper's domain, consisting of sitting room, still room and steward's dining room. The china was kept in cabinets in the West Corridor.

The 'decorator' more than anyone else set the scene in the house. Frank Copcutt (who later became the head gardener) was perhaps the best decorator that Nancy had and was always careful to take account of Nancy's taste for mixed flowers. On some occasions he would alter the arrangements in the house three times a day.

Nancy's orders were transmitted through the heads of department: the butler, the housekeeper and the chef. Lee travelled in a car between the Astors' houses, rather than in the van that sufficed for the other servants. His specific duties included delivering letters, locking the house at night and selecting and serving the wine. People meeting Lee pigeon shooting in the grounds at Cliveden when the family were away frequently mistook him for Lord Astor. Lee would often not be told how many people there would be to a meal and occasionally resorted to listening in on selected telephone conversations when he felt the caller was likely to be invited:

I remember on one occasion her ladyship saying there would be eight. 'And Lee,' she said, 'don't make the table too big. No luncheon can be a success with the guests too spread out.' I made arrangements accordingly. Her ladyship went out for the morning. At one o'clock, not only did the eight guests arrive, but sixteen others. The sixteen were the members of some women's organisation and among them were well-known people like Mrs Lyttelton and Miss Tankerville. I phoned the Chef: 'There are sixteen extra people for lunch. Can you manage?' 'How can I manage?' said he. 'The food won't go round.' I said: 'You've got eggs. Make omelettes. And salads with cold meat.' He set to work. Her ladyship did not arrive back till a quarter past one. She was astounded to see so large a party. 'I didn't ask you for today,' she said to Miss Tankerville. 'It was tomorrow you were to come.' 'No, it wasn't,' returned Miss Tankerville, 'it was today you said.' 'No, I didn't,' said her ladyship. A set to of this sort always put

her ladyship in good spirits. She said to me: 'Can the cook do it, Lee?'
'Give me ten minutes,' I replied. Her ladyship took the twenty-four guests
to the drawing-room, where laughing and teasing them she kept them
amused. In ten minutes I announced: 'Luncheon is served.' It was an
excellent lunch, with plenty for all. That sort of thing often happened.[30]

The housekeeper's staff was comparable in its size to the butler's: there were
four or five housemaids and a sewing maid in the 1930s. The housemaids had
a tough routine, starting work at 5 a.m. and cleaning the house by hand.
(Vacuum cleaners were not brought in until after the Second World War.)
Everything had to be in order before breakfast at 9 a.m. Two important female
members of staff did not come within the purview of the housekeeper: Nancy
Astor's maid and the children's Nanny.

THE DAILY ROUTINE

Rose Harrison started work at Cliveden in 1928 as Waldorf's and Nancy's
daughter Wissie's lady's maid. Lee described Nancy Astor to Rose: 'She is not
a lady as you would understand a lady, Miss Harrison ... you won't find her
easy.'[31] Rose, a tough Yorkshire woman, understood plain speech and was not
daunted by Nancy's domineering ways. In fact, when she became Nancy's
personal maid in 1930 she gave as good as she got and remained in service at
Cliveden until Nancy's death in 1964. Rose felt she was expected to work
eighteen hours a day, seven days a week and commented, 'no matter what
you did for her, she never let you see she was pleased'.[32] The routine was that
at 7.30 in the morning Rose collected Nancy's clothes from the night before
from her dressing room. At 8 o'clock Rose
called Nancy with a tray of coffee and fruit,
Nancy then spent half an hour reading the Bible
and the Christian Science publication *Science
and Health*. This was 'doing the lesson'.

Nancy's main work in the morning was with
her secretary, answering letters, issuing
invitations and writing out notes for a speech,
but before this the children had to be given their
lesson. From an early age Nancy impressed on
the children that in some respects they would
be lucky if they survived the rest of the day
without disaster if they neglected this part of

*Rose Harrison.
The photograph was taken
shortly after she started
work at Cliveden in 1928.
She became Nancy Astor's
personal maid and was
undaunted by Nancy's
domineering ways. She re-
mained with her until
Nancy's death in 1964.*

*Mr Lee, the butler.
He started work at
Cliveden in 1912 and
stayed until 1960. It was
Lee who ensured the
efficient running of the
household.*

their duties. Michael Astor wrote:

> *With children she was in her element. From her they met with something quite different from the usual set of instructions passed on to them by parents and nannies. The average grown-up, when faced with a child – his own or someone else's – will, in self defence, remember the cardinal rule which is: 'Don't get it over-excited.' My mother's approach was a more positive one. Her idea was to make it laugh. She scored success after success... This was her age group: the very young and wholly unselfconscious. With anything in between the age of innocence and the fully-matured creature her performance often misfired.*[33]

Waldorf also loved his children and at about seven in the morning they would visit while Lee was shaving him, and one of them might sit on his knee. When Waldorf took the morning lesson the children found it much less exciting.

Christmas in the Great Hall at Cliveden. Now, as then, Christmas is celebrated with great style.

CHRISTMAS AT CLIVEDEN

Joyce Grenfell, Nancy's niece, has left a wonderful account of Christmas at Cliveden in her childhood:

We usually arrived on Christmas Eve in the dark at tea-time, the car sent to fetch us from Taplow Station loaded with our baggage and the parcels Tommy and I were not supposed to notice. 'Mummy, what's in that?' 'Wait and see – it's Christmas.' As we turned the corner by the giant marble shell fountain, at the end of the straight quarter-mile approach to the house, the glassed-in porch as if by magic suddenly blazed with light. How did anyone know we were coming? I only discovered years later that when a car passed through the main iron gates of the park the lodge-keeper telephoned, on a hand-wound private line, to warn the house that it was coming. The butler was at the open door to greet us. 'Shake hands with Mr Lee'. We did and said we were quite well, thank you, to him and to the footmen waiting to carry in the bags. We shook hands, too, with the parlourmaid, hovering behind them, in her dark brown alpaca uniform with a gossamer-fine organdie apron, high collar, and head bandeau cap tied with brown velvet ribbon.

Joyce Phipps (later Grenfell) in 1929, at the age of nineteen, on the tennis court in the Forecourt at Cliveden.

Stepping into the porch they sniffed the special Cliveden smell that came from pots of humea. As well as tennis racquets there were hockey-sticks and golf bags, and a giant Chinese jar full of golf-umbrellas and walking sticks.

In the front hall we saw the giant Christmas tree was where we expected it to be, at the foot of the oak staircase. The banisters were festooned with garlands of box, yew, bay, ivy, holly and other evergreens that, as well as the humea, gave off a subtle aromatic scent. Only once were we allowed to help decorate the tree. The job was usually done by a gardener on a step-ladder, with the housekeeper handing him the tinsel and coloured balls. I always made sure that certain favourite decorations were still there; the glass birds in little tin cages were regulars I looked for.

Nancy, wearing golf socks and ghillie's shoes, came out to greet them.

'You children go on upstairs – and take your coats with you. I will not have them left all over the place.' She was rather fierce, and, after kissing her proffered cheek and feeling, as always, as if I had done something wrong, I scrambled up the polished stairs.
'Come on down right away as soon as you have washed. You needn't change today. Tea's ready...'

They came down and sat at the children's table near the fire, where Waldorf would join them, pouring out their milk and slicing the bread and plain cake specially baked for them.

At the grown-ups table, where Aunt Nancy presided, there were delectable little scones in a lidded silver dish, kept hot over a spirit lamp. There was also a special, almost black, rich fruit-cake topped with marzipan, chocolate éclairs and very short crisp shortbreads, all made in the still-room by two full-time cake-and-pastry-cooks. Sometimes we were allowed special treats from the grown-ups' table, but Aunt Nancy kept an eye on the goodies and we were strictly rationed.

When tea was over, Nancy went to her present-room, which was a small dark panelled study next to her boudoir.

No child was allowed to go there, particularly at Christmas-time, but, once when I was about sixteen and was sent in there to fetch something for her, I saw it was like a little shop. Piles of sweaters of all colours and sizes, men's, boys', women's and girls'; silk stockings, silk scarves, chiffon squares and boxes of linen handkerchiefs, from the Irish Linen Stores, initialled for everyone in the party. There were evening bags, men's ties, golf-balls in boxes, little packs of tees, diaries, toys, games, books and candy. Lots of candy. There was never a more generous present-giver than Aunt Nancy, but she was always careful about her candy store; most of it came from American friends, and she didn't let it out of her keeping except in very occasional bestowals of a caramel here and a sour-ball there. She also had a great many boxes of chewing-gum and was never without a supply in her pocket. Presents from the store were given to everyone in the house, family, friends, staff and visiting staff – in those days ladies' maids and valets always accompanied their employers. Aunt Nancy's private secretary helped by doing much of the present buying, and all the

*wrapping up in layers of best quality tissue-paper tied with inch-wide red
satin ribbon. Aunt Nancy wrote the tags.*

At about half-past six the bell-ringers and carol-singers arrived. All Joyce
remembered of the carol singers was:

> *... a small group of men and boys in dark clothes; one a hooty tenor who,
> before the group joined in, swooped through an opening solo verse of* See
> Amid The Winter Snows *with all the notes run together. This, for some
> reason, gave me bad church-giggles. Wissie caught it. The boys became
> infected, too. Aunt Nancy gave us fierce frowns. It happened every year. I
> half-hoped, half-dreaded the swooper would swoop again; and every year
> he did it.*

Later they were sent upstairs to bed, on their way stopping at their uncle's dressing room, where his valet had put out a selection of stockings to choose from.

> *As very small children we didn't open our stockings until we took them to
> our parents' room, and there in their bed we discovered what it was that
> crackled and tinkled and bulged so enchantingly... Nursery breakfast was
> upstairs. After giving us all time to go to the bathroom and 'be good', and
> after waiting for our parents to finish their breakfast in the dining-room,
> we were allowed to go downstairs.*

In the front hall a transformation had taken place:

> *On every chair, all over the sofa and on the big high-backed oak bench by
> the fireside, were piles of presents. Everyone, grown-ups and children, had
> a pile marked with his or her name.*
>
> *The noise in the front hall was deafening. New bicycles had bells to
> ring, toy motors had hooters. We all screamed a great deal.*
>
> *'Look – oh, look what I've got!'*
>
> *Of course we were spoiled and given too much of everything. If the
> giving had been limited only to those who already had, it would have been
> indefensible, but my aunt and uncle were sharers on the grand scale with
> all and sundry, and their imaginative generosity, undiscovered for the
> most part, was their special gift. And not only at Christmas.*

Piling into several cars, they were driven to the little hillside church at
Hedsor for Morning Service.

Waldorf Astor with the Oxford Draghounds in the Forecourt at Cliveden *by Alfred Munnings.*

The great thing about Christmas at Cliveden was the way the pattern was adhered to. We could count on the day's shape remaining the same. After presents, church and luncheon, we were made to go out, whatever the weather, for air and exercise. About two-thirty in the afternoon of Christmas Day, everyone, grown-ups and children (that made it more fun for the children) went down to the immense lawn below the terrace, to the south of the house. Sides were picked and we played 'French and English'. Darkness fell early. We went back to the house, and Aunt Nancy said: 'You all get your books and sit quietly for an hour.'

As they grew older, they were allowed to stay up for dinner. On Christmas night they wore fancy dress.

At Cliveden dressing up for Christmas-night dinner was a big excitement. On the first floor, called the French Landing, there was a large black-and-gold Chinese chest, and in it was kept a tumbled collection of dressing-up clothes. Some were genuine fancy dresses. There was an exquisite white taffeta Pierrette costume, decorated with fluffy black pompons, made for Aunt Nancy to wear, when she was a bride, to the famous ball at Devonshire House, some years before the 1914 War.

After dinner there were charades, and people did turns. Aunt Nancy's annual and favourite turn was always a success. She borrowed Uncle Waldorf's pink hunting-coat, white breeches and shiny black boots, jammed his black velvet huntsman's cap (too big) well down over her small face and became a little 'Nouveau Riche' hunting-man, rising – with his imaginary wife, 'my Rosie' – up the social scale. Snobbish? Yes. Funny? Very! In this disguise she was entirely possessed, improvised after-dinner speeches, danced in character, walked in character and conducted dialogues with my mother, who 'fed' her, that held us all entranced. We came to believe in the reality of the little man...

Years later Aunt Nancy invented other characters. She got hold of a set of 'prop' plastic teeth and was unrecognizable, and became an upper-crust British woman with prejudices against Abroad and 'Emmericans'; and until within a few years of her death at eight-two, she could turn herself into one of those gallant women (her exact contemporary) who served in the WAAC in World War I, and show how some twenty-eight years later this heroine marched in the peace parade after World War II. This old girl, with knees bent, stoop exaggerated and head thrust forward, lurched by, giving the salute to an invisible Personage on a dais. It was funny, tragic and admirable, at all levels.

The children never quite understood what was being laughed at, and they became sleepier and sleepier, and quieter and quieter, so that ten-thirty and eleven passed without their presence being noticed. Then, 'oh joy, *midnight*. And so to bed.'

'Goodnight, and thank you, Aunt Nancy.'
'Have you had a happy Christmas?'
'Rath-er – and thanks awfully for my presents.'

Then slowly upstairs, where the rouge I had applied over-generously didn't shift with soap and water, so I left it on and fell into bed. Awful to think Christmas was over. But – oh good – Boxing Day tomorrow...[34]

OUTDOOR ARRANGEMENTS

The estate was practically self sufficient: milk came from White Place Farm across the river, vegetables from the kitchen garden and flowers from the greenhouses. Wages were paid on a different basis for indoor and outdoor staff. The indoor servants were usually unmarried and lived in the house until they married, when they often left the Astors' service. Most of the outdoor staff lived with their families in cottages. Servants received much of their remuneration in kind (free accommodation and meals, together with certain allowances such as beer and laundry money). The outdoor staff got a wage, out of which they had to pay the rent for their houses.

Because Cliveden was some way from the nearest villages, the Astors' created a social life for those who worked for them. 'The Club' at Cliveden was presided over by Lord Astor, and Cliveden had its own football and cricket teams. The staff used the tennis court and the golf course when the family was away and on alternate weeks there would be a dance or a whist drive. Two big days of the year were the summer party, which was a fête with a flower show and knitting and needlework displays, sports accompanied by the Maidenhead Silver Band and all the fun of the fair for the children of the estate, ending with a big dance in the evening. The other big event was the Christmas party. In the evening there was the fancy-dress dance that the family attended and at which the staff let down their hair. Rose Harrison's prize-winning fancy-dress outfit was as Eliza Doolittle in 'Eliza Comes to Stay', and Arthur Bushell, Lee's number two, dressed as a lady Christian Scientist, with an involuntary facial twitch.

Waldorf built up a modern dairy at White Place Farm (with one of the first tuberculin-tested herds), but his greatest passion was horses, and he formed a famous stud, starting when he was still at Oxford. From four thoroughbred mares – Conjure and Popinjay were two of them – all the racehorses in his stud were to descend. Between 1907 and 1950 Waldorf's horses won 460 races, to the value of £487,570, and were placed second and third in 547 other races. Wins included such classic races as the Oaks, Two Thousand Guineas, One Thousand Guineas and St Leger. It was a great disappointment that Waldorf never won the Derby. Nancy wrote:

Five times I have had to watch his horse come in second. After the fifth time, when we were driving home, he said to me: 'Never mind. The great thing is the children are well.'[35]

In the early days horses provided all the transport, but by the 1920s they were kept only for recreation and exercise. Transport was in the hands of the garage department, run by four chauffeurs who kept careful records of their activities. For example, in 1938 Mr C. Hopkins maintained the Phantom II Rolls Royce and did approximately 17,000 miles; Mr A. Jeffries looked after the Rolls and the Humber Landauette and travelled 12,000 miles. The garage department in that year cost £ 2,000, and the cars travelled 88,000 miles, at a cost of five and a half pence per mile.[36]

A Summer Evening, Cliveden by Alfred Munnings. Waldorf is seated on a shooting stick, with the mares and foals at the Cliveden Stud. His groom, Mr Guy, well known in the racing world, stands behind him. The painting hangs at Cliveden.

THE ENDING OF AN ERA

The staff ensured that Cliveden ran like clockwork, but for the Astors themselves life was changing. During the 1930s Waldorf and Nancy began to diverge politically, he to the Left and she to the Right, and to lead more separate lives. Nancy was possessive to a destructive degree, particularly as a mother. The children suffered from her suffocating affection, and there were numerous confrontations as Nancy tried to direct the course of every aspect of their lives. This inevitably had the effect of driving her children one by one away from her and from Cliveden, a fact that Nancy bitterly resented and never understood.

In 1937, for the first time, there was no Christmas party at Cliveden. Waldorf and Nancy went to Florida, and for the children the heart was going out of family gatherings.

Joyce Grenfell was lent Parr's Cottage at Cliveden in the 1930s and 1940s, and her letters to her mother show that she sensed the changing atmosphere in the big house. In December 1940 she wrote:

> When one hasn't been to C. for a while its strange restlessness smites you, I find. Too much goes on. Too many people, too much talk, too much food. The fires are lovely, so are the flowers and it is fun in some ways but oh, how glad I am to get down to my quiet little drawing room, with my books and Brahms First Symphony.[37]

In another letter written three months later she recorded:

> It's always struck me as significant that Uncle W. escapes to the somewhat chill but ever happy atmosphere of his Munnings-hung room upstairs![38]

It was at this time that Waldorf and Nancy faced a new and much more public problem, one that was to make the name of Cliveden known throughout the world. During the 1930s the rise of the Nazis in Germany gave increasing cause for concern, but views differed as to how this threat should be tackled.

THE CLIVEDEN SET AND HITLER'S WAR

The 'Cliveden Set' was the name given to a supposed group surrounding the Astors who were considered to be pro-German, and pro-appeasement with Hitler. The phrase was the invention of a Communist intellectual named Claud Cockburn, who published several stories about the Cliveden Set in *The Week*, his four-page mimeographed news-sheet, which was distributed by hand but

A cartoon by Low in the London Evening Standard *in 1938 showing Nancy Astor and members of the so-called 'Cliveden Set', who, at the time, were believed to have greatly influenced British foreign policy towards appeasement with Germany.*

travelled widely by word of mouth. It was after a specially dramatic story on 17 November 1937 that the idea of the Cliveden Set took off 'like a rocket'. Cockburn claimed that the Astors were head of a cabal and that Cliveden was acting as an unofficial Foreign Office.

In March 1938 the Communist Party printed a penny pamphlet entitled *Hitler's Friends in Britain*, which sold 20,000 copies and announced on its cover:

> *From Cliveden House in Buckinghamshire operates the Cliveden Set –*
> *making and breaking British Cabinet Ministers – bringing Britain to the*
> *verge of War – wielding the power of International Fascism.*

A look through the Cliveden Visitors Book for the 1930s makes a nonsense of the Cliveden Set conspiracy theory. The anti-appeasers stayed at Cliveden as frequently as the appeasers, and the weekend parties were never exclusively representative of one faction or the other. There is not a single weekend where all the guests could be considered to have been appeasers. However, in

NOTICE
All American journalists meeting the Prime Minister at lunch must use invisible ink
Nancy Astor

A cartoon by Wyndham Robinson showing a somewhat bemused Prime Minister, Neville Chamberlain, being interviewed by American journalists, with Nancy Astor on the left as the 'invisible link'.

people's minds the Cliveden Set became fixed as those who were in favour of appeasement whether they were known to the Astors or not. The myth went marching on because it first dramatized and then summarized a whole vague body of suspicions and fears.

There *was* a 'Cliveden Set' of those who visited Cliveden, but they were certainly not all of the same mind and, as Cockburn later wrote in his autobiography, 'they would not have known a plot if you had handed it to them on a skewer...'[39] One of Nancy's closest friends, Lord Lothian, was indeed a fervent appeaser, and the Prime Minister, Neville Chamberlain, was their friend. Many influential people gathered (as they always had) under the Astors' hospitable roof: such men as Lord Halifax, the Foreign Secretary, Sir Neville Henderson, the new British Ambassador to Germany, and on one occasion the German Ambassador, Herr Von Ribbentrop.

The Astors' inclination was to ignore the Cliveden Set publicity. They thought it too preposterous for any thinking person to take seriously. However, in March 1938 when Waldorf and Nancy returned from a visit to America, where a *New York Times* headline proclaimed 'Friends Of Hitler Strong In Britain' and the *Washington Post* announced 'Astor Country Home Becoming Real Centre of Foreign Policy', Waldorf and Nancy realized that remaining silent would only add fuel to the fire. Thereafter they both did what they could to expose the myth.

Waldorf wrote to leading newspapers at home and abroad, on 5 May 1938 sending a letter to *The Times* debunking the whole idea of the Cliveden Set. He explained, truthfully, that he and Nancy had for years 'entertained in the country members of all parties (including Communists), members of all faiths, of all countries, and of all interests'. He pointed out that a crucial house party in January 1938, at which important decisions were supposed to have been taken, never happened – Cliveden was closed, the Astors were in America and Lord Lothian was in India. Waldorf ended his letter, 'The whole conception of the "Cliveden Set" is a myth from beginning to end', but in the tense atmosphere of those days the legend gave a simple explanation for a situation that was deeply alarming and accepted as true.

Nancy sent out to those who had enjoyed the hospitality of Cliveden over the years group photographs in which they featured with the note, 'Cliveden Weekends have become so World Famous that you might like to have a photograph of one which you graced with your presence.'[40]

The sacrifices of the First World War were still too painful a memory for any British Government to ignore the overwhelming hope that another world war could be averted. Where people differed was over how long this hope was tenable. From 1936 onwards Hitler perpetrated a series of outrages, yet nobody thought they justified another world war. Winston Churchill was one of the few voices in Parliament to warn the nation that Hitler's hidden agenda made a cataclysm inescapable. In September 1938 came the Munich Conference, at which Neville Chamberlain met Hitler in an attempt to negotiate a peaceful outcome to the Sudeten question. A friendship agreement was signed on 30 September and Chamberlain returned home announcing, 'Peace with Honour'. (It was during that month that Waldorf quietly removed his valuable paintings from St James's Square to the safety of Cliveden.) Chamberlain was received with wild public enthusiasm and by almost everyone in the House of Commons. An exception was Winston Churchill, who made one of his great speeches. Nancy Astor interrupted him frequently, and her hostility during the debate produced a wave of bad publicity in the United States. At about the same time Charles Lindbergh told the world that the German air force was unbeatable, received a decoration from Hitler and was entertained by the Astors. These events prompted Frederick Collis to write in the widely read American magazine *Liberty* that the Cliveden Set was a disgrace to Britain.

Nancy turned to her Marxist friend, the eighty-three-year-old G. B. S. to defend her. Shaw responded in the April 1939 edition of *Liberty*:

Cliveden is like no other country house on earth. Mr Collis' list of noble conspirators is authentic; but you meet these aristocrats at Cliveden because you meet everybody worth meeting, rich or poor, and of every point of view. You meet the Duchess of Atholl; but then you meet also Ellen Wilkinson, the Leftist member of the Labour Party in Parliament. You meet Colonel Lindbergh, the friend of Herr Hitler's Chief of Staff; but you meet also Mr Charles Chaplin whose dislike of Nazi rule is outspoken to a degree which must seriously threaten his interests in Germany. You meet the Marquess of Londonderry, descendant of Castlereagh and so far to the right that he was too much for even the existing Nationalist Cabinet with his famous majestically beautiful wife; but then you meet also ME, an implacable and vociferous Marxist Communist of nearly sixty years standing with MY beautiful wife. If I wanted, I could prove that Cliveden is a nest of Bolshevism or indeed of any other sort of bee in the world's bonnet.

He ended, 'Never has a more senseless fable got into the headlines.' Nancy came to her own defence in an article 'Lady Astor Interviews Herself', published on 4 March 1939 in the *Saturday Evening Post*:

... we do not entertain with any plan or plot. With a purpose, yes, for our life has a purpose; but not a plot or plan. I am too impulsive to plot or even to plan long ahead. Naturally, we entertain politicians, and politicians include peers and paupers. But they are only some of the guests. They're mixed up with Labor men, social workers, writers, our American friends, religious teachers, temperance workers – all sorts... I believe the world moves on by putting together all kinds of honest minds. The object of our parties is just that – to give people of all sorts a chance to get together and hear one another's views.

She ended, with considerable justification:

My compatriots must have lost their sense of the ridiculous if they swallow this nonsense about my directing cabinet policy, but I am supposed to have more power than had Queen Elizabeth, Marie Antoinette and Cleopatra combined.

Although the Astors and their friends cannot escape the blame that attaches to all those people, prominent or ordinary, who supported the British Government's policy of appeasement, the suspicion that Nancy and her friends supported that policy for sinister reasons and were powerful enough to direct the cabinet was an hallucination born of a deeply troubled hour.

On 14 March 1939 Hitler invaded Czechoslovakia, thus making a mockery of all the promises he had given to the British and the French at Munich. The British public finally realized how futile their hopes of curbing Hitler's territorial ambitions had been. Two days later Nancy rose at Prime Minister's Question Time in the House of Commons to ask, 'Will the Prime Minister lose no time in letting the German Government know with what horror the whole of this country regards Germany's action?' Vyvyan Adams, a Conservative Member of Parliament, immediately rose and said, 'You caused it yourself', thus giving

The visit of Queen Elizabeth and the Princesses Elizabeth and Margaret to the hospital at Cliveden in the Second World War. Nancy Astor is seated on the right.

fresh impetus to the Cockburn legend. Waldorf speaking in the House of Lords on 13 April made a confession of error but pointed out that he was not alone:

> *I think we should all be big enough to admit that during the past year or two each of us and all of us as individuals and as parties have probably made some mistakes. I do not think it would be possible to find anybody whose record, whose forecast, whose foresight had been completely correct.*

It was Germany's invasion of Poland on 1 September that made war inevitable. Two days later Britain and France declared war on Germany. Hitler, however, still dismissed England's resolve, perhaps partly because of the enormous publicity given to the fable of the Cliveden Set. The entry in the diary of Dr Goebbels (Hitler's propaganda Minister) for 3 September is revealing and prophetic: 'He [Hitler] thinks there will be only a phoney War in the West. But now I know that Churchill is in the Cabinet, I cannot believe that.'[41]

The Astors' error was the same as that of the British Government and Opposition: to believe that Hitler could be restrained without the use of force. It was an error without sinister motives, and their delusion was shared by most British people.

Nancy the Appeaser became Nancy the Fighter, a fact the Nazis must have realized as after the war it was discovered that Nancy was on the Nazi 'Black List' of people to be arrested as soon as the Germans occupied London. Her son David, the most anti-Nazi member of the family, believed this may have been because of her disrespectful treatment of Ribbentrop on an occasion he witnessed. This was a lunch party, given by Nancy at 4 St James's Square in 1937, when she told Ribbentrop that England would never take Hitler seriously as long as he wore his Charlie Chaplin moustache. Ribbentrop was not amused.[42]

In August 1939 Waldorf greatly reduced the number of staff at Cliveden, and the Canadian Red Cross again set up a hospital there. Waldorf, whose health was deteriorating (he suffered a mild stroke in 1942), spent much time at Cliveden. Life there was a mixture of visits from celebrities, such as G. B. S, who mingled with busy nurses and convalescing soldiers. They all enjoyed the 'entertainments' provided by Nancy and Joyce Grenfell, who had then just embarked upon her stage career.

In the darkest days of the war, Waldorf considered the future of Cliveden. He saw that the beginning of the war marked the end of an era, and he realized that life would never be the same again. Joyce Grenfell also saw this clearly and wrote in November 1940 to her mother about the young Astors and their friends at Cliveden:

> *The more I see of people brought up in the easy way the more I lean*
> *towards socialism. I needn't worry; we're hurtling in so called – or*
> *comparatively – easy stages towards it. Things will never, can never,*
> *mustn't ever be the same, as they were before the war.*[43]

Waldorf's concerns in relation to Cliveden were the cost of upkeep, current taxes and future death duties. This was coupled with the fact that conflicts within the Astor family meant that the house was no longer a focal point for his children.

The Astors' close friend Lord Lothian had given Blickling Hall and its contents to the National Trust on his death in 1940. He had also left the four and a half thousand acres of land surrounding the house. Thus Blickling Hall became the first house to be accepted with an endowment of land under the National Trust's new country house scheme, which had itself been initiated by Lord Lothian.

Philip Kerr, 11th Marquess of Lothian, was a lifelong friend of Nancy Astor and a member of the group known as the 'Cliveden Set'.

Waldorf wished to preserve Cliveden and its (much smaller) estate for all to enjoy in the same way and decided to give Cliveden to the National Trust with immediate effect. He had already made an agreement to protect the Thames reach of the Cliveden Estate. This 'Private Open Space Agreement' of July 1929 ensured that the beautiful stretch of land bordering the Thames would never be built over.

The gift to the National Trust included the house and estate, and a monetary endowment needed for its upkeep, together with many of the furnishings in the house that related to the history of the place. These included the portraits after Lely of the 2nd Duke of Buckingham and his mistress, the Countess of Shrewsbury; the Philip Mercier painting of Frederick, Prince of Wales, and his three sisters at Kew; the wonderful Sargent portrait of Nancy Astor; the Alfred Munnings painting of Lord Astor with his mares and foals. The Astors' did not reserve any legal interest in the property but agreed with the National Trust that the family should be left in occupation as long as they wished to remain. If they left the house, it should be 'used for promoting friendship and understanding between the peoples of the United States and Canada and the other dominions' in much the same way as it had been used by Waldorf and Nancy. At the same time as the Astors' gift, the Canadian Red Cross and the Canadian Government agreed to give the Canadian Military Hospital buildings and their equipment to the National Trust at the end of the war.

The gift of Cliveden was widely welcomed. Vincent Massey, High Commissioner for Canada, was quoted in *The Times* on 9 December 1942, the date of the announcement:

> *Lord Astor has done a very generous and imaginative thing, and his action will be appreciated nowhere more warmly than in Canada. Many Canadians, in this War as in the last one, have become familiar with the charm and beauty of Cliveden through the ever-present hospitality of its owners, and will be very glad to hear that its amenities are now to be safeguarded for all time.*

In fact, during the Second World War, Nancy's and Waldorf's energies were directed more to Plymouth, where Nancy was the Member of Parliament and Waldorf was appointed Lord Mayor, with the backing of all political parties, which was a great personal tribute to him. Their courage and determination during the appalling bombing raids on the city were legendary.

During the war Waldorf sensed the mood in the country for a different social order after the conflict was over, and his own radicalism loosened his links with the Conservative Party. It was mainly because of this that he decided that his 'socialist' son David (rather than his eldest son Bill) should eventually take over *The Observer* newspaper.

SEPARATE LIVES

This decision drove Waldorf and Nancy further apart both politically and emotionally. Nancy was never one to hide her feelings and spoke of her anger with Waldorf. Without her husband's restraining hand Nancy's political performance, both inside and outside the House of Commons, was becoming highly erratic and a public embarrassment.

At the end of the war in September 1945 Nancy had been in the Commons for twenty-five years and was sixty years old. Waldorf, after careful consideration and discussion with his sons, asked Nancy not to stand for re-election to Parliament. For Nancy this was a bombshell and she only complied with his wishes as a 'dutiful wife', very much against her will.

The effect on their relationship was initially straining and ended by being devastating. For a few months Waldorf went away to stay, first with his stepson, Bobbie, then with David, and when he returned to Cliveden Nancy went to their house in Sandwich (built in 1911 for golfing holidays). This was to be the pattern of their lives for the next few years. Waldorf behaved with great gentleness and patience, and in the numerous letters he wrote pleading for a return to normal relations it is clear that he never lost his love and respect for her.

They did manage two visits to America together, but on the occasions they were in the same house Nancy's vitriol was never far from the surface. The final blow for Nancy was when David took over the editorship of *The Observer* in 1948. She attacked the paper in public and threatened to return to public life. The ageing Waldorf inevitably found this very draining.

In August 1952 Waldorf had a heart attack while staying with David. He knew the end was near and insisted on returning to Cliveden because, he said, 'It would distress your mother if I die anywhere else'. Waldorf returned

to Cliveden and was installed in his bedroom, which was now on the ground floor. Nancy returned to be with him for the last days of his life. These moments must have been poignant for them both, and after Waldorf died Nancy grieved for 'the years wasted'. At a lunch party soon after she said to her neighbour, 'You know, he was no good without me, and alas, I am no good without Waldorf.'[44]

Michael Astor wrote about his father:

He was such a good and trusting man that people who met him wanted to know him better. He was not easy to get to know, and he had no small talk of any kind. His modesty and uprightness conveyed their own meaning and men, after meeting him, often came away feeling reassured, because his own qualities of integrity and decency were ones he sought to establish in others.[45]

Waldorf's last words to each of his children individually were, 'Look after your mother'. They did so in spite of the difficulties her possessiveness had made for

Waldorf, 2nd Viscount Astor (1879-1952), a photograph by Bassano of 1935. Relations with Nancy were strained during the last seven years of his life, but they were together at Cliveden during his last days. After his death, Nancy grieved for 'the years wasted'.

Satyr Resting, a marble statue in the Rose Garden. The garden was designed for Bill Astor in 1959 by Geoffrey Jellicoe.

them. Bill told his mother that she could stay and run Cliveden for as long as she wished. She did so for a short time but realized that it was too much for her, and she spent her remaining days at Hill Street in London and Rest Harrow in Sandwich.

THE THIRD VISCOUNT ASTOR

History repeated itself when Waldorf's death brought to the end his son Bill's career in the House of Commons. Bill and Nancy had been the first mother-and-son partnership there. Bill now devoted himself to charity work. He also spent time improving the grounds at Cliveden and created the Rose Garden, which he asked Sir Geoffrey Jellicoe to design. He also replanted large areas of beech wood along the cliffs above the Thames. One of Bill's additions to Cliveden soon after taking over was a swimming pool in the Walled Garden. Bill and his brother had frequently asked their mother about building a pool, but she was happy swimming in the Thames and answered calls for a pool with, 'No, no its disgustin' I don't trust people in pools.'[46]

Bill was determined to bring some of the pre-war life back to Cliveden. He entertained on a lavish scale (but there was much less attempt at putting the world to rights than in his parents' day). One of the most spectacular social events was the coming-out dance for Douglas Fairbank's daughter, Daphne, on 18 June 1957. There were 450 guests including the Queen and Prince Philip, Princess Margaret, the Duchess of Kent and Princess Alexandra. Tony Armstrong-Jones, a young photographer just beginning to make a name for himself, took the photographs.

Bill was generous and hospitable to a fault, and had a mass of friends and acquaintances, but he did not always choose them wisely. This was especially so in the case of Dr Stephen Ward.

STEPHEN WARD AT SPRING COTTAGE

In 1949 Bobbie Shaw had recommended an osteopath to Bill after a fall out hunting led to constant back pain. Stephen Ward's treatment proved to be a great help to Bill and, because Ward was an amusing companion, a friendship developed. Ward had an impressive list of clients, to which he was continually adding, partly through his skill with the portraits he drew in

Spring Cottage on the banks of the Thames, rented by Dr Stephen Ward from 1956 to 1963. Ward used the cottage for weekend parties, entertaining such guests as Christine Keeler and Mandy Rice-Davies.

pastel. Ward not only enjoyed manipulating people's limbs but also their lives. This was often achieved by introducing influential men to the beautiful young women with whom he surrounded himself.

During the hunting season Ward made regular professional visits to Cliveden, so got to know the place well. In the summer of 1956 he noticed a run-down cottage bordering the Thames. Spring Cottage derived its name from a mineral spring that had been turned into a small spa by the Countess of Orkney in 1813. This had become part of a building designed by George Devey for the Sutherlands in 1857. Ward asked Bill whether he could rent the cottage for use at weekends. Bill agreed to lease it to him at a peppercorn rent, on the condition that Ward would be readily available to give treatment to Bill and on occasion his guests. Ward's move into Spring Cottage coincided with Bill's second and short-lived marriage to Philippa Hunloke. Bill asked Ward to help effect a reconciliation, which was unsuccessful, but it created closer bonds of friendship between them.

In 1960 Bill married Bronwen Pugh, a beautiful twenty-eight-year-old model. She loved Cliveden and was a superb hostess. Bill's third marriage was very happy. Bronwen's modelling friends had warned her about Stephen Ward and when she met him she instinctively felt that he was trouble. Bill brushed aside her apprehensions, with tragic consequences.

Ward's behaviour became increasingly bizarre. He enjoyed the low life and the high life, and the sexual antics he organized at Spring Cottage and in London were part of the manipulation that gave him power over people. He had clear instructions as to what he was allowed to do at Cliveden. He could use the swimming pool (as could some of the other tenants and neighbours), but only after checking that it was convenient. Apart from his professional visits, the number of times he was entertained at the house (particularly after Bronwen's arrival) were limited.

It was the weekend of 8 and 9 July 1961 that put the name of Cliveden across the newspapers worldwide for the second time in the century – but this was not to happen for another two years.

CHRISTINE KEELER AND THE JULY WEEKEND

Bill had invited a mixed group of people in much the same way as his parents had always done. The first guests arrived on Friday night. John Profumo, Secretary of State for War for the past year, and his wife, the actress Valerie Hobson, were the earliest on the scene. A further nine guests came on Saturday for the night and others, including Nubar Gulbenkian and Lord Mountbatten, came to lunch and dinner. The president of Pakistan, General Ayub Khan, came for lunch on Sunday.

Stephen Ward also had a house party for the weekend. Two of his guests at Spring Cottage were Christine Keeler, just nineteen and full of sexual magnetism, and Captain Yevgeny Ivanov, an assistant Soviet naval attaché who was also a spy reporting daily to the GRU (the main intelligence directorate of the Soviet Army). Ward was politically left wing and saw himself as playing a significant role in East-West relations during a particularly tense period of the Cold War. His friendship with Ivanov fitted this scenario well, and it was perhaps no coincidence that Ivanov was invited to Spring Cottage that particular weekend.

It turned out to be the hottest weekend of the summer, and on Saturday night Ward and his guests were somewhat noisily enjoying the Astors' pool. After dinner Bill and his party in dinner jackets and evening dresses strolled

The swimming pool in the Walled Garden, installed by Bill Astor. It was here, in July 1961, that a chance meeting took place between Christine Keeler and John Profumo, Secretary of State for War.

out of the *porte-cochère* towards the Walled Garden. Bill and Jack Profumo (as he was always known) went through the door into the garden ahead of the party to find Ward and his guests, one of whom, Christine Keeler, was topless. The embarassed Christine ran to the far end of the pool just as the rest of the Astor party arrived. It was Valerie Profumo who came to her rescue by handing her a towel. Some of the party went for a swim, and when they returned to the house Ward and his guests were invited to join them. Bill Astor stated (privately) that nothing worthy of comment happened at the pool or in the house. However, eighteen months later Christine sold a highly coloured account of the episode to the tabloid press for a large sum of money. As this was the only published report, it was accepted as 'fact'. She claimed, among other things, that Bill and Profumo had chased her naked around the pool while Ward grabbed her costume and threw it in. Bill, she claimed, then switched on the floodlights so that the party could watch the proceedings.

On Sunday after lunch Ward's party returned to the pool, this time accompanied by Ivanov. Christine's version of events (published later in the *News of the World*) was that they had all played a series of games, including a wrestling match in which each man with a girl on his shoulders attempted to topple the opposing couple. Profumo and Christine were one of the couples. It is not known what went on that afternoon, but there is no doubt that Profumo was very attracted to Christine. Ivanov, in his autobiography written over thirty years later, recorded that Profumo was 'flirting outrageously with the young girl'.[47]

Later in the afternoon Ward asked Ivanov if he would drive Christine back to London as he had to treat Bill's back before returning to town. Ivanov wrote about the car journey, 'She was clearly pleased with her success with Lord Astor and Jack Profumo... But I noticed with surprise that she was also trying to use her charms on me.'[48] When they arrived at Ward's flat, Christine asked Ivanov in for a cup of tea. Ivanov claimed:

> *What happened next became the subject of speculation for many years afterwards, as if it mattered as far as the Profumo affair was concerned if I had slept with Christine or not. I am prepared to admit now that I did. I allowed Christine to seduce me. That devil of a girl could seduce anybody!*[49]

Christine later described Ivanov as 'A great big huggy bear'. Thus the weekend ended with Ivanov and Christine in bed together – probably for the only time. Shortly afterwards Profumo and Christine began a three-month affair.

Ivanov felt that Bill Astor could be a useful source of information to him and the GRU. Ward persuaded Bill to invite Ivanov to lunch at Cliveden. The Russians were worried about how to contain the movement of German citizens from the East to the West without the NATO countries and America stepping in to protect the free movement of citizens.

THE FOREIGN OFFICE IS INFORMED

Bill thought his meeting with Ivanov and Ward sufficiently interesting to report it to the Foreign Office in a letter written on 2 August. The reply stated, 'The Russians are making a particular effort at present to estimate public opinion about the Berlin crisis and to find indications of dissension amongst the Western Allies.'[50] Four days later the Berlin Wall began to be built.

An even more serious crisis came about a year later, in October 1962, when Khrushchev sent nuclear missiles to Cuba. Kennedy demanded their removal.

Ivanov was instructed to do what he could to open up unofficial channels that might lead to the start of negotiations between East and West as Khrushchev now wanted to extricate himself without loss of face. Ward again asked Bill for his help, this time in arranging for Ivanov to meet the journalist Lord Arran. This was followed by a dinner at Cliveden on 27 October, during which the news of Khrushchev's withdrawal came through. Ivanov was astounded by this turn of events.

POLICE INVESTIGATIONS

Nothing more would have been heard of that July 1961 weekend at Cliveden and all that happened later had it not been for something that occurred six weeks after the Cuban missile crisis. Christine Keeler's rejected West Indian lover fired pistol shots at Ward's house, where Christine was staying. The police in their investigations inevitably unearthed unsavoury details of Ward's life and the fact that he was in touch with MI5.

The press hounded Christine, who decided that she could benefit at least financially from her uncomfortable situation. She agreed to write a series of articles for the *Sunday Pictorial*, which would include her version of events at the Cliveden weekend. Ward alerted Bill Astor, who instructed his solicitors to contact the newspaper. Bill also warned Profumo of what was in the air.

The publicity about the case alarmed the security forces, who felt that Ward's intelligence activities might be revealed in court, so they decided that their best course of action was to discredit him. The police, with difficulty, put together a case against Ward, which was that he 'knowingly lived wholly or in part on the earnings of prostitution'.

Ivanov had by now been sent back to Moscow. The publicity attracted the interest of politicians and in particular the Labour Member of Parliament George Wigg, who was on the Opposition

Above: A pastel drawing of Christine Keeler by Stephen Ward that hangs at Cliveden. Left: Stephen Ward with Christine Keeler on the right.

Front Bench. He had always disliked Profumo and saw that the connection between Profumo and Ivanov via Christine Keeler could be interpreted as constituting a serious security risk. This was a situation that not only could be used to embarrass the Government but even to bring about its downfall. The Labour Party was to achieve its goal in spite of the fact that Lord Denning's famous report on the affair, published in September 1963, stated that there had been no breach of national security.

The daily revelations in the press, both true and false, made it inevitable that Profumo would have to make a statement in the House of Commons. He did so on 22 March 1963 and categorically denied that there was any impropriety in his relationship with Christine Keeler. The truth could not be suppressed for long, and once his lie was exposed he had to resign. His own political career was over. Seven months later the Prime Minister, Harold Macmillan, resigned, and the Labour Party's reward came in the following year when they ousted the Conservatives and held power for the rest of the decade. George Wigg was made Paymaster General.

THE END OF THE PROFUMO AFFAIR

Ward's trial opened at the Old Bailey on 22 July 1963 and lasted for eight days. The testimony (much of which was subsequently discredited) of various prostitutes was reported by the world press, which revelled in the titillating details of perversion, voyeurism, orgies and drugs. Ward remained calm throughout the case. It was only the summing-up of the judge, Sir Archie Pellow-Marshall, that broke Ward's spirit. He felt that the judge had made the outcome of the trial inevitable and that he had become an Establishment scapegoat. At the end of that day he returned to the flat where he was staying and took an overdose of Nembutal. He left a note for his host:

> *It is really more than I can stand – the horror, day after day at the Court and in the streets... am sorry to disappoint the vultures...*[51]

The next day the judge decided that the case should continue, even though Ward was in a coma, and he carried on with his summing-up. The jury then withdrew to consider their verdict. Ward was found guilty on two of five counts, on what was shown later to be slender and faulty evidence. Several days later, and before sentence was passed, Ward died without regaining consciousness.

Bill Astor was throughout the whole unhappy business vilified by the press and accused of deserting his friend Ward. He was, in fact, one of the few people

Bill Astor with his third wife Bronwen and the Astor children, William (the present Viscount), Emily, Janet and Pauline, on the terrace outside Nancy Astor's bedroom.

who had stood by Ward, and had given him money to cover his legal and living expenses. Bill was never asked to appear as a witness by either the prosecution or the defence, but the fact that he did not appear was given a sinister interpretation by the press. During the trial one of the main witnesses, Mandy Rice-Davies, claimed Bill Astor had been one of her lovers. When it was pointed out to her in court that he, through his counsel, had denied this, she replied with a phrase that has since entered the language, and the *Oxford Dictionary of Modern Quotations*, 'He would, wouldn't he?'

Bill's mother was now eighty-two-years old, and friends and relations went to ingenious lengths to keep the newspaper reports of the trial from her. They also arranged for people to telephone every day just before the one o'clock and six o'clock radio news. This worked well until she went to stay with her son David at Sutton Courtenay. One morning she rose early and read the newspapers. At breakfast she announced that she was going to Cliveden to be seen at Bill's side as she was determined to stand by her son. Nancy's memory was poor by this time and on the way she asked David, 'Why are we going to Cliveden?' David explained that it was to see Bill. 'Why am I going to see Bill today?' she asked.

THE LAST OF THE ASTOR YEARS

Nancy was only vaguely aware of the notoriety that had engulfed her beloved Cliveden. She died on 2 May 1964. The last word she uttered before lapsing into a coma was 'Waldorf'. Her ashes were taken to Cliveden and placed in the same tomb as her husband, in the Octagon Temple. At her request the casket was covered by the Confederate flag that had been given to her in Danville, her birthplace.

It was for friendship, not love, that Nancy had genius. Bill commented that in order to enjoy affection with her as a mother one 'had to first kill one's love'; his brother Michael wrote:

Her public proclamations, her militant postures, were forever in her life contradicted by her irresistible human touch. Her love and recognition of people was the special gift she had to make which she bestowed on quite unsuspecting people who, at one moment, met her as strangers; and at the next discovered they had found a new sort of friend. This was the gift that had so enhanced my father's life. [52]

The Astors' lives were shattered by the Profumo Affair. Bill carried on with his work for refugees around the world, but his heart problems had undoubtedly been exacerbated by the stress and strain, and his health deteriorated rapidly. Although his family and close friends were loyal and supportive, Bill's 'fair weather friends' publicly deserted him. His wife Bronwen remembers:

It was like living a nightmare. There was an awful silence... I remember we would turn up at functions and people would literally turn their backs and walk away from us. [53]

Bill Astor died two years after his mother, in March 1966, at the age of fifty-eight. In the spring of the following year Bronwen left Cliveden for good. Bill's son William Waldorf, by his first wife Sarah Norton, became 4th Viscount Astor at the age of fourteen. Bill's death left the family facing massive death

The herbaceous border in the Forecourt designed by Graham Stuart Thomas for the National Trust in the 1960s. The door leads to the Walled Garden, which contains the swimming pool.

duties as, although he had made gifts to his heir, he had not lived the requisite number of years to make the gifts absolute. The family had considered moving from Cliveden during Bill's lifetime (mainly because the house was open to the public); after his death they decided that remaining at Cliveden was not practical and told the National Trust that they wished to move out.

Cliveden was about to enter another, very different, period in its already colourful history.

*Overleaf:
The Water Garden and Chinese Pagoda.
The Pagoda was made for the Paris Exhibition of 1867 and was bought by William Waldorf at the sale of Bagatelle, Lord Hertford's villa in the Bois de Boulogne, in 1900.*

CHAPTER IX

Stanford University

CLIVEDEN 1969–1983

STANFORD UNIVERSITY of California took a lease of Cliveden for use as one of its overseas campuses in 1969. The 'New Cliveden Set', as one local newspaper described it, remained there for the next fourteen years, fostering understanding between peoples of the English-speaking world as the Astors had specified. Stanford was one of the first major American universities to develop the concept of overseas study centres for its undergraduates, and it did so on a scale unprecedented in American higher education at that time. During the 1970s about half of all Stanford undergraduates spent six months living and studying at one of the overseas campuses in Austria, France, Germany, Italy or England. Bob Walker, Director of Stanford's overseas campuses, stated in the introduction to a report produced in 1969:

> *Stanford's aim in presenting the opportunity to study in a foreign country is to make it possible for every student who wishes to do so to have an introduction to life in a foreign environment and culture. This is part of liberal education in its best sense and all members of the Stanford academic community agree that it helps develop new perspectives and insights in its students, especially toward themselves and toward their own American culture.*[1]

He ended, 'For each student participating study in another country becomes his own "voyage of discovery".'

This was put more colourfully in a report, *Stanford in Britain*, written for students in 1973:

Students of Stanford University 'on campus' at Cliveden in the 1970s.

Stanford University students playing tennis in the Walled Garden with the nineteenth-century Water Tower in the background.

Where else can you swim in Christine Keeler's swimming pool before breakfast...or listen to lectures in Lord Astor's billiard room?...At Stanford in Britain you literally live inside a piece of English history.[2]

There were usually eighty students living at Cliveden at any one time, including thirty or so women occupying the top floor of the main house. After protests in the mid-1970s male students began to be given rooms on the top floor; this apparently annoyed some of the women, who resented being expelled to the former Service (West) Wing, where the male students lived along with the numerous staff (principally the dining-room staff and cook: there was also a housekeeper, who lived in Gas Yard Cottage).

Visiting Stanford faculty members and their families lived in style on the first floor of the main house. The Academic Director, Sir Jack Rumbold, later Chairman of the Industrial Relations Tribunal, occupied the Chinese Bedroom, and the other rooms in the East Wing were used by the Director of Administration, G. A. B. Docker, and the administrative staff. The main lecture theatre was in the former billiard room (now the Mountbatten Bedroom); the Canning Bedroom was used as a seminar room and the Sutherland Bedroom as a guest room for visiting academics. The former Drawing Room (now the Terrace Dining Room) was used as the main library, Lady Astor's boudoir as the Senior Common Room and the main hall as a common room for everyone. The French Dining Room was out of bounds, except when receptions were held for the local community. Students, staff and faculty ate communally and substantially in the former servants' hall in the basement, and there was a gloomy subterranean bar in the former footmen's room, presided over by the resident barman, Jim Reeve.

The academic curriculum consisted of courses in British literature, history and politics, and related subjects. These were taught by visiting academics from local universities and from Stanford's home campus, and the three resident tutors, and some students also went to Reading and Oxford for individual tutorials. The work counted towards the students' final degree.

The students' workload was not unduly heavy, with lectures from nine o'clock to midday and again in the afternoon. There were frequent field trips, including regular week-long excursions to France and Italy, until budget cuts intervened in the mid-1970s. The academic year was divided into two sessions: January to June and June to December. At first, all students came for six months.

The Drawing Room was extensively remodelled by Waldorf Astor. He introduced the bookcases, fireplaces and overmantels. This shows the Stanford students using the room as a library.

During Stanford's time at Cliveden some 2,000 students studied there. The report *Stanford in Britain* ended:

> *Cliveden is rhododendrons in the Spring, and Water Garden blooms in all colors. It is the piano late at night and the Library for studying during papers and finals, for reading Shakespeare, Bertrand Russell, John Ruskin, D. H. Lawrence and Edmund Burke with a new sense of the people and the country they wrote about.*[3]

There was a lively cultural life, with plays, concerts of Baroque music and even, for a brief period, a feminist Nancy Astor Affinity Group. Generations of Stanford students left Cliveden with warm feelings towards the house and towards England in general, which have remained with them; two students even got married there. But the comfortable country house ambience gradually came to be criticized as unsuitable for the intellectually challenging programme set by what by the early 1980s had become one of the leading universities in the world. One student summed up the weakness of Cliveden as an educational centre: 'We were pretty isolated at Cliveden, but I made it to many pubs to rap with the English.' The isolation and inevitable country-club atmosphere it fostered, coupled with the image of a transplanted Californian Beach culture, which Stanford was at pains to eradicate, prompted the university to move to Oxford in 1983. Stanford in Britain still flourishes there in a row of High Street houses leased from Magdalen College.

For the National Trust, Stanford University was a happy partner in terms of international understanding, but the students were hardly ideal as far as the fabric of the house and its contents were concerned. Visits from the Stanford football team caused occasional damage, including in one instance the stopping of the clock in the tower and the removal of doors from their hinges. Filling the house with student dormitories and utilitarian furniture was clearly not doing Cliveden justice, and after Stanford moved the National Trust hit upon a perfect solution for the house.

Stanford University students on the Parterre at Cliveden.

*Overleaf:
The* Suzy-Ann,
a beautifully restored 1911 pinnace, on the Cliveden Reach of the Thames, with the house in the background. The launch is one of the flotilla used by guests of the Cliveden Hotel.

CHAPTER X

Cliveden–Hotel Extraordinary

CLIVEDEN 1985 – THE PRESENT

THE NATIONAL TRUST advertised the lease of Cliveden in 1984 and the brochure stated on its cover that this was 'A unique opportunity to lease one of England's finest stately homes, suitable for a number of alternative uses, subject to planning, including office, institutional, educational and residential. Approximately 38,500 sq ft net.'

The many enquiries explored all the suggested uses and more. One idea that had not been mentioned was proposed by three groups, which was that Cliveden could be turned into a hotel. The National Trust were impressed by this suggestion as it was a use that was much in sympathy with the terms of the original gift by the Astors in 1942. William, 4th Viscount Astor, was an enthusiastic supporter, later becoming a director of the hotel company.

The proposal presented by Cliveden PLC (as the company was subsequently named) won the day principally for two reasons. Firstly, the Chairman John Lewis and the Managing Director John Tham had earned accolades and awards for converting another Grade I listed building into a luxury hotel – the Royal Crescent Hotel in Bath. Secondly, the plans of the architect, William Bertram, showed that the conversion of the main house could be achieved with virtually no structural alteration, with the former's dressing rooms becoming large bathrooms, providing the services and comfort expected by today's hotel guests.

However, for the National Trust to grant a forty-five-year lease of a Grade I listed building for a hotel was to set a precedent. There was also anxiety about how the idea of a luxury hotel – almost certainly beyond the means of most

Right:
The north front of Cliveden, designed by Charles Barry in 1850. In the foreground is Thomas Waldo Story's Fountain of Love. According to Waldorf Astor's note of 1920, 'the female figures are supposed to have discovered the fountain of love, and to be experiencing the effects of its wonderful elixir.'

202

Trust members, even though part of the house would be open on two afternoons a week – would be received. In the event, the Thames & Chilterns Regional Office of the National Trust received only one complaint. The effect of the letter was somewhat lessened by the writer expressing the hope that Cliveden would be pulled down because of 'all the wicked events' that had taken place there in recent years.

CLIVEDEN HOTEL AND THE NATIONAL TRUST

The work carried out by Cliveden Hotel on the interior and the National Trust on the exterior of the building has been as extensive as that carried out by William Waldorf, 1st Viscount Astor, and the close and effective partnership between landlord and tenant has ensured that any problems have been discussed and resolved as they have occurred. The West Wing was the only part of the house that required radical reorganization. This servants' wing had been a jumble of small rooms, but it contained one important original feature: Thomas Archer's staircase (see page 39). It was, however, awkwardly placed, and eventually it was agreed that the staircase could be successfully resited in the new layout for the West Wing.

Cliveden Hotel's major contributions came with the second and third phase of the work. These were in the rundown Walled Garden and surrounding area, which contains the famous swimming pool, and in the dilapidated stable

The Walled Garden in 1985, and as it is today, showing the Pavilion for the indoor pool and treatment rooms built by the Cliveden Hotel.

The Club Room, created in 1994 in the old stables and making use of the original stalls. It is used by members of the Cliveden Club.

courtyard. At the north end of the Walled Garden is the Pavilion, built in 1990, which contains a large heated pool and several treatment rooms. This stucco building in a classical style was designed by William Bertram in collaboration with John Tham, John Lewis and Julian Harrap, the National Trust's architect. The building has been successfully broken down into three pavilions to create a simple and elegant structure, which, because of its hi-tech servicing, is the most complex at Cliveden.

The south side of the Walled Garden is bordered by Henry Clutton's Bothy Wing, which had inappropriate additions of red brick lean-to buildings. The Bothy used to contain stables with staff quarters above. The external restoration and the restructuring inside have made space for six additional bedrooms and the Churchill Boardroom, which is filled with all the modern equipment required for company meetings. This building has been renamed the Garden Wing (see page 121). Another part of Clutton's building which joins the Garden Wing on the south side also contained stables and servants' rooms. This has been

The Churchill Boardroom in the Garden Wing, equipped with the most up-to-date technology for high-level meetings.

redesigned to add another six bedrooms and a further boardroom making the total number of bedrooms thirty-seven. These rooms have been beautifully panelled in oak in a style that was popular in Clutton's time.

On the ground floor the Duke of Westminster's personal stables, which had become badly run down, have been restored and are now used by the Cliveden Club, members of which enjoy all of Cliveden's facilities at special rates throughout the year. In the Club Room each stall has been adapted to make a dining area for six people. The room is full of humorous touches: the table legs are in the shape of horses' legs and hooves; the bar stools are saddles.

The numerous different materials used in the building of the house created conservation problems, the most difficult of these being the reconstruction of Barry's complex roof. He could have used a pitched roof on the main house, as exists on the East and West Wings, but instead he designed a flat roof, the surface of which was made up of fine-looking Penrhyn slates from Wales. These were supported on another slate structure standing on a barrel vault that in turn rested on a steel frame. The whole roof structure was four feet thick. Barry's construction was ahead of its time and was only in a poor state of repair because there were no reliable mastics available in 1850. Barry clearly wished to create a 'promenade deck' on the roof and after a skilful reconstruction it is now again possible to walk on the roof and to enjoy the magnificent view to the *Fountain of Love* and, in the opposite direction, down the Parterre and beyond to Windsor Castle.

Right:
The French Dining Room today, a superb eighteenth-century setting for the private parties that are regularly held here.

The considerable investment required for conversion and improvement by Cliveden Hotel led to the granting of a new lease from 30 October 1990, which runs for one hundred years from 1985. This means that Cliveden Hotel's tenure will be the longest in the history of the house, and Cliveden is becoming known as a beautiful hotel with a historic past.

THE HOTEL

Cliveden has been a focus of attention throughout its history. When it opened as a hotel in March of 1986, an article in *The Times* was headed 'An Internationally Famous Hotel Two Weeks Before Opening', an indication of the strength of the media coverage that the conversion of Cliveden received.

The philosophy for the running of the hotel was carefully developed by John Lewis and John Tham and their team. Their approach was to run the house as the Astors had in its Edwardian heyday. The interior design of the public areas by Rupert Lord set the scene; John Lewis and the author added to the collection of paintings, concentrating on works relating to the house and its owners.

John Tham, together with the first Manager, John Sinclair, and his team, put this philosophy into effect and created an atmosphere that sets Cliveden apart from other hotels. Turning the pages of the visitors book in each room confirms this. For many guests the experience of

Pages from the visitors books that are placed in each suite or bedroom in the hotel. The page on the right depicts the gales of October 1987.

208

The Sutherland Bedroom contains furniture dating from the Duke and Duchess of Sutherlands' time at Cliveden. Each bedroom or suite is named after an owner of the house, or an architect or visitor connected with Cliveden. There is also a room named for the Astors' butler Mr Lee.

staying is 'the experience of a lifetime', or 'unforgettable' or 'unique'. Some entries are almost essays; some are poems or drawings. Most are in English but others are in Japanese, French, German, Spanish or Italian.

There are numerous entries to show how much pleasure Cliveden is giving to people in its present incarnation; indeed, some guests have returned to the house again and again, staying in a different room on each occasion.

There is a staff of three per bedroom and there is still a butler, housekeeper, footmen and housemaids. Mr Lee, the Astor's butler, was replaced by Mr Holiday as the *éminence grise* of the staff hall. As in the past, guests relax, or they can play tennis or squash, go riding, jogging or boating on the Thames; they can swim in one of the pools, and be massaged and manicured and generally cosetted.

The Canning Bedroom in the East Wing, one of several panelled bedrooms at Cliveden.

The long Terrace Dining Room is the largest of the three dining rooms and has a superb view down the Parterre. Downstairs is Waldo's Restaurant, which has been beautifully panelled and, in 1993, the chef, Ron Maxfield, was awarded a Michelin star for his cuisine.

PRESENT-DAY ENTERTAINING AT CLIVEDEN

Cliveden has always been the perfect setting for parties, and now there are more parties than ever. One of the most flamboyant was the birthday party given by Sir James Goldsmith for his wife Annabel on 11 June 1987, which turned out to be election night. The house and grounds were beautifully floodlit, and three bands were flown in from New Orleans to play in a large, magnificently decorated tent on the West Terrace.

The most spectacular anniversary party celebrated the 250th anniversary of the first performance of 'Rule, Britannia' at Cliveden (described in Chapter III). The evening of 1 August 1990 was warm and crystal clear, the Royal Philharmonic Pops Orchestra, conducted by Antony Hopkins, performed pieces by Walton, Elgar and Saint-Saëns with enthusiasm. 'Rule, Britannia' was sung by Sarah Walker, famous for her rendering of the song at the Promenade Concerts. As the sky darkened, the full moon travelled in an arc over the orchestra on the Parterre. The stars became visible, and the evening ended with a wonderful display of fireworks accompanied by Handel's 'Music for the Royal Fireworks'.

The Terrace Dining Room,
(formerly the Drawing
Room), redecorated in
1995. The fine portrait by
Reynolds of Miss Horneck
(bottom left) was
purchased by William
Waldorf Astor and was
given to the National
Trust to hang in the room
by Waldorf's son David in
1994. The portrait over
the mantelpiece (bottom
right) is of William
Waldorf by Herkomer.

Royal visits to Cliveden have taken place regularly since the Duke of Buckingham's day, and the tradition continues. H.R.H. The Princess of Wales has been twice as guest of honour for charity balls, and H.R.H. Princess Margaret came as guest of honour on another occasion. Princess Margaret remembers being somewhat intimidated by Nancy Astor until her nephew encouraged her to stand her own ground. The first occasion she did so, Nancy was delighted and said 'Atta Girl!'[1]

Cliveden is a favourite venue for honeymoon first-nighters. Apart from the attractions of the house, and the attentiveness of the staff, Heathrow is nearby for a getaway the following day. Numerous wedding receptions take place and some marriage blessings: actors Kenneth Branagh and Emma Thompson celebrated their marriage at Cliveden. In November 1991 the present Viscount Astor's half-sister Janet married the Earl of March, heir to the dukedom of Richmond and Gordon. The marriage was blessed in the Octagon Temple and was followed by a reception. Many members of the Astor family were there and all were impressed with how the old atmosphere of Cliveden had been retained. Elizabeth Winn, a great-niece of Nancy Astor, remarked, 'I was sure Aunt Nancy was going to poke her head around the door and exclaim in her Virginian drawl, "what d'all doin here?".'[2]

All those now involved with Cliveden can answer Nancy Astor's hypothetical question. The partnership of conservation and commerce has produced an ownership and a *modus operandi* for the house that works for the building and for the guests. It is a use of which Nancy Astor would surely have approved.

After ten years Cliveden has achieved a pre-eminent position and become the highest-rated hotel in the United Kingdom. The magic of Cliveden continues to work its spell on both its visitors and those who work there. Cliveden is flourishing in this latest chapter of its fascinating history.

The Nancy Astor Bedroom, which overlooks the Parterre; one of the grandest suites in the Hotel.

NOTES TO THE TEXT

References are to works listed in the Select Bibliography

CHAPTER I

1. Leland, p. 29
2. Macky, p. 57
3. Fairfax, p. 8
4. Evelyn, pp. 176-7
5. Fairfax, p. 8
6. Burnet, i, pp. 171, 172
7. Fairfax, p. 4
8. Ibid, p. 6
9. Pope, p. 153
10. Villiers (1715), i, pp. 137, 138
11. Hamilton, pp. 122, 201
12. Ibid, p. 201
13. Pepys, p. 27
14. Ibid
15. Hertfordshire Record Office, Cowper MS Panshanger D/EPF49, quoted Pritchard, p. 160
16. Quoted Fairfax, p. 10
17. Pepys, p. 201
18. Fairfax, p. 10
19. Quoted Burghclere, p. 164
20. Reresby, p. 71
21. Quoted Wilson, John, p. 126
22. Ailesbury, p. 13
23. Dryden, pp. 177, 178
24. Christie, pp. 105, 106
25. Royal Commisssion on Historical Manuscripts, p. 36
26. Quoted Wilson, John, p. 191
27. Royal Commission on Historical Manuscripts, p. 36
28. Ibid
29. Ibid
30. Ibid
31. Villiers (1715), i, p. 148
32. Quoted Drake, p. 269
33. Evelyn, pp. 98, 99
34. British Museum, Harley MS 7003, f. 272
35. Ibid
36. British Museum, Additional MS 27872, f. 34
37. Villiers (1715), i, pp. 185, 186
38. Blakeborough, p. 72
39. Pope, p. 153
40. Buckingham's Commonplace Book, G.L.C. Record Office and History Library, p. 90

CHAPTER II

1. Swift, x, p. 315
2. Royal Commission on Historical Manuscripts, Portland MS, iv, p. 266
3. Dalton, p. 38
4. Swift, iii, p. 103
5. Ibid, p. 165
6. Ibid, p. 115
7. Johnson and Chalmers, p. 22
8. National Library of Scotland, MS 1033, ff. 14, 14a
9. Macky, p. 57
10. Campbell, p. 4
11. National Library of Scotland, MS 1033, f. 15
12. Ibid, f. 157
13. Transcript made by John Craster, one of Lord Orkney's executors: Northumberland Record Office, Craster Papers, ZCR9
14. Lewis, p. 266
15. British Museum, Extracts from the Diary of Sir Jeremiah Milles, Additional MS 15776
16. Markham, Sarah, pp. 177-8
17. *London Gazette*, 6301, 7 September 1724
18. Croker, pp. 350-2
19. Dalton, p. 38

CHAPTER III

1. Barr, p. 140
2. Hervey, p. 262
3. Quoted in full Walters, p. 221
4. The household accounts of Frederick, Prince of Wales, in the Duchy of Cornwall Archives, are bound in twenty-two volumes; this quote, viii, p. 355
5. Hervey, p. 79
6. Quoted Scott, p. 386
7. Vertue, i, p. 14
8. Cust, pp. 46, 47
9. Dodington, p. 23

10. Ibid, p. 23
11 Royal Library, Windsor
12. Quoted Walters, pp. 206, 207
13. Quoted Walters, p. 218
14. Stanhope, p. 1705
15. Curties, p. 293

CHAPTER V

1. National Trust, Hughenden Manor, Bucks
2. Letter dated 21 May 1847 to Very Revd: John Lee, Principal of Edinburgh University; National Library of Scotland, MS3445, f. 284
3. Warrender Letter Book, Letters 1836-40, collection Lord Bruntisfield
4. Gronow, p. 339
5. Warrender *Autographs of Peers* (one of the Letter Books)
6. Ibid
7. Thorne, p. 494
8. Bagot, p. 20
9. Croker, p. 82
10. Warrender *Autographs of Peers*
11. Ibid
12. Ibid
13. Ibid
14. Ibid
15. Castle Howard archives

CHAPTER VI

1. Greville, p. 19
2. Leconfield, p. 33
3. Gower (1884), p. 59
4. Ibid, p. 1
5. Barry, p. 120
6. Staffordshire Record Office, D593K/1/3/43, 18 January 1855
7. Clutton's account, November 1859, Staffordshire Record Office, Sutherland Accounts, D593/K/1/10/14
8. Ibid, 3 May 1858
9. Ibid, 23 March 1861
10. Pevsner, p. 98
11. Gower, p. 13
12. Ibid, p. 14
13. Fleming, pp. 29, 30
14. Ibid, p. 22
15. Castle Howard archives, F7/18

16. Hervieu, p. 4
17. Gower, p. 107
18. Earl of Carlisle's diary, 25 June 1852, Castle Howard archives J19/8/29
19. Gladstone, v, p. 398
20. Ibid, p. 490
21. Ibid, 213
22. Ibid, p. 267
23. Ibid, p. 271
24. Gower, p. 111
25. Ibid, p. 12
26. Martin, p. 245
27. Queen Victoria's Journal, Royal Library, Windsor
28. Fulford, p. 75
29. Royal Library, Windsor, R.A. Vic. Add. A/24/377, 378
30. Queen Victoria's Journal, Royal Library, Windsor
31. Gower, p. 198
32. Morley, p. 197

CHAPTER VII

1. Gower, p. 16
2. Huxley, p. 66
3. Queen Victoria's Journal, Royal Library, Windsor
4. Ibid
5. His entry in *Dod's Parliamentary Register*, quoted Huxley, p. 69
6. Quoted Huxley, p. 100
7. Ibid, p. 101
8. Ibid, p. 72
9. Ibid, p. 197
10. Ibid, p. 197
11. Ibid, p. 143
12. Ibid, p. xii
13. Grosvenor Estate archives, City of Westminster Archive Department
14. Huxley, p. 129
15. Ibid, p. 141

CHAPTER VIII

1. William B. Astor's Obituary in Frank Leslie's *Popular Monthly*
2. Cowles, p. 148
3. Astor, Michael, pp. 17, 18

4. Cowles, p. 153
5. Full account appeared in *The Sun*, 7 February 1898. General Owen was a close friend of Edward VII and was present with him at the Tranby Croft house party in 1890 when one of the party was accused of cheating at cards. This led to the famous Baccarat Scandal
6. Quoted Cowles, p. 154
7. Note made by Pauline Astor on 16 September in her 1896 photograph album
8. Astor, William Waldorf, p. 213
9. Ibid, pp. 61, 62
10. Quote from David Astor, who told the author (18 June 1992) that William Waldorf Astor spoke to Nancy and not to his son Waldorf, as recorded in Collis, p. 32
11. Quoted Sykes, p. 92
12. Ibid, p. 98
13. Langhorne, p. 37
14. Pakula, p. 130
15. Quoted Sykes, p. 149
16. Quoted Sykes, p. 162
17. Quote from the Bridgeman papers in the Shropshire Record Office given to the author by Dr Cameron Hazlehurst of the Australian National University, Canberra
18. Quoted Sykes, p. 127
19. Quoted Astor, Michael, p. 128, from a short essay written by Walter Elliot for Michael Astor in 1955
20. Churchill, p. 55
21. Sykes, p. 296
22. Patch, p. 59
23. Knightley and Simpson, p. 240
24. Cowles, p. 186
25. Quoted Collis, p. 46
26. Astor, Michael, p. 79
27. Ibid, p. 63
28. Quoted Sykes, p. 148
29. Recounted by Nigel Nicolson in conversation with the author (2 November 1985) concerning a conversation Nicolson had with Harold Macmillan
30. Collis, pp. 37, 38
31. Harrison (1975), p. 46
32. Ibid, p. 39

33. Astor, Michael, p. 68
34. Grenfell (1979), pp. 190-8
35. Quoted Collis, pp. 39, 40
36. *General Report of Garage Department for 1938*, three-page typescript, Astor archives, Reading University Library, MS 1066/1/333
37. Grenfell (1988), p. 190
38. Ibid, p. 203
39. Cockburn, p. 21
40. Wilson, Derek (1993), p. 271
41. Dr Goebbels' Diaries, transcribed by David Irving and edited by Peter Millar, quoted in the News Review section of the *Sunday Times*, 12 July 1992, p. 3
42. David Astor in conversation with the author (18 June 1992)
43. Grenfell (1988), p. 187
44. Quoted in *Nancy*, Westwood Production for ITV, 7 November 1979
45. Astor, Michael, p. 218
46. Elizabeth Winn in conversation with the author (5 October 1993)
47. Ivanov, p. 69
48. Ibid, p. 70
49. Ibid
50. Wilson, Derek (1993), p. 383
51. Knightley, p. 245
52. Astor, Michael, p. 217
53. Knightley and Kennedy (1987), p. 257

CHAPTER IX

1. Stanford Archives, Oxford, made available by Geoffrey Tyack
2. Stanford Archives, *Stanford Overseas Campuses* (1973/4)
3. Ibid

CHAPTER X

1. H.R.H. Princess Margaret in conversation with the author (27 March 1990)
2. Elizabeth Winn in conversation with the author (22 May 1992)

ORKNEY FAMILY TREE

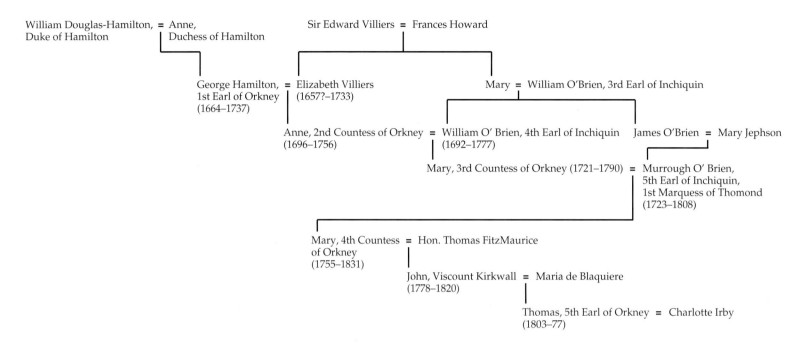

ASTOR FAMILY TREE

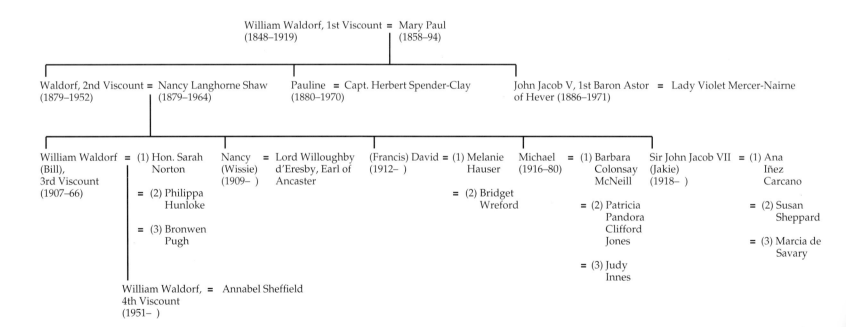

THE ASTOR HOUSEHOLDS, 1928

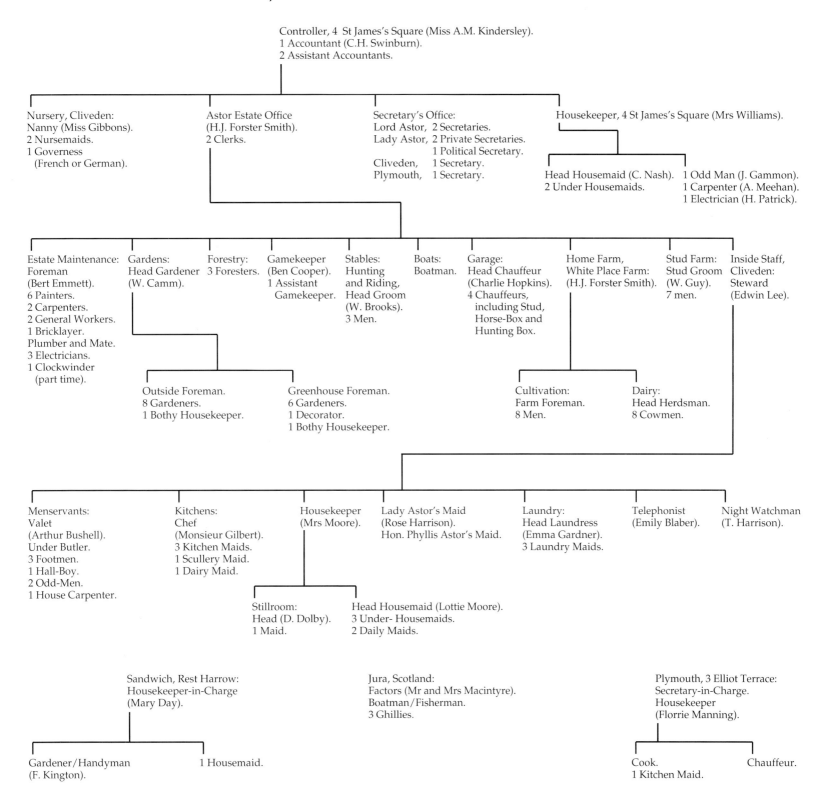

Controller, 4 St James's Square (Miss A.M. Kindersley).
1 Accountant (C.H. Swinburn).
2 Assistant Accountants.

Nursery, Cliveden:
Nanny (Miss Gibbons).
2 Nursemaids.
1 Governess
  (French or German).

Astor Estate Office
(H.J. Forster Smith).
2 Clerks.

Secretary's Office:
Lord Astor,   2 Secretaries.
Lady Astor,   2 Private Secretaries.
              1 Political Secretary.
Cliveden,   1 Secretary.
Plymouth,   1 Secretary.

Housekeeper, 4 St James's Square (Mrs Williams).

Head Housemaid (C. Nash).
2 Under Housemaids.

1 Odd Man (J. Gammon).
1 Carpenter (A. Meehan).
1 Electrician (H. Patrick).

Estate Maintenance:
Foreman
(Bert Emmett).
6 Painters.
2 Carpenters.
2 General Workers.
1 Bricklayer.
Plumber and Mate.
3 Electricians.
1 Clockwinder
  (part time).

Gardens:
Head Gardener
(W. Camm).

Forestry:
3 Foresters.

Gamekeeper
(Ben Cooper).
1 Assistant
  Gamekeeper.

Stables:
Hunting
and Riding,
Head Groom
(W. Brooks).
3 Men.

Boats:
Boatman.

Garage:
Head Chauffeur
(Charlie Hopkins).
4 Chauffeurs,
including Stud,
Horse-Box and
Hunting Box.

Home Farm,
White Place Farm:
(H.J. Forster Smith).

Stud Farm:
Stud Groom
(W. Guy).
7 men.

Inside Staff,
Cliveden:
Steward
(Edwin Lee).

Outside Foreman.
8 Gardeners.
1 Bothy Housekeeper.

Greenhouse Foreman.
6 Gardeners.
1 Decorator.
1 Bothy Housekeeper.

Cultivation:
Farm Foreman.
8 Men.

Dairy:
Head Herdsman.
8 Cowmen.

Menservants:
Valet
(Arthur Bushell).
Under Butler.
3 Footmen.
1 Hall-Boy.
2 Odd-Men.
1 House Carpenter.

Kitchens:
Chef
(Monsieur Gilbert).
3 Kitchen Maids.
1 Scullery Maid.
1 Dairy Maid.

Housekeeper
(Mrs Moore).

Lady Astor's Maid
(Rose Harrison).
Hon. Phyllis Astor's Maid.

Laundry:
Head Laundress
(Emma Gardner).
3 Laundry Maids.

Telephonist
(Emily Blaber).

Night Watchman
(T. Harrison).

Stillroom:
Head (D. Dolby).
1 Maid.

Head Housemaid (Lottie Moore).
3 Under- Housemaids.
2 Daily Maids.

Sandwich, Rest Harrow:
Housekeeper-in-Charge
(Mary Day).

Jura, Scotland:
Factors (Mr and Mrs Macintyre).
Boatman/Fisherman.
3 Ghillies.

Plymouth, 3 Elliot Terrace:
Secretary-in-Charge.
Housekeeper
(Florrie Manning).

Gardener/Handyman
(F. Kington).

1 Housemaid.

Cook.
1 Kitchen Maid.

Chauffeur.

SOURCES

The Duke of Buckingham's Commonplace Book is in the Greater London Record Office and History Library (together with other papers deposited by the Earl of Jersey); the British Library has documents and letters to and from Buckingham. The National Library of Scotland, Edinburgh, holds the correspondence between the Earl of Orkney and his family. The account books of Frederick, Prince of Wales, are in the Duchy of Cornwall Archives, London; there is also manuscript material in the Royal Library, Windsor. The correspondence between the Countess of Orkney and Mrs Piozzi is in the John Rylands University Library of Manchester. Sir George Warrender's Letter Books belong to Lord Bruntisfield, his descendant. The Sutherland archives are held by the Staffordshire Record Office; the Royal Library, Windsor, has Queen Victoria's diaries and letters. The Grosvenor Estate archives, including some material relating to Cliveden, are held by the City of Westminster Archive Department, London. The principal collection of material relating to the Astors is in the Reading University Library; in 1985 the National Trust deposited Cliveden papers in the Buckinghamshire County Record Office, Aylesbury, and there is also material at the Thames and Chilterns Regional Office of the National Trust at Hughenden Manor, Buckinghamshire.

SELECT BIBLIOGRAPHY

Ailesbury, Thomas, *Memoirs of Thomas, Earl of Ailesbury*, i (London, 1890)
Astor, Gavin, *Hever in the Twentieth Century* (privately printed, 1974)
Astor, Michael, *Tribal Feeling* (London, 1963)
Astor, Nancy, 'Lady Astor Interviews Herself', *Saturday Evening Post* (4 March 1939)
Astor, William Waldorf, *Pharaoh's Daughter and Other Stories* (London, 1900)
Aulnoy, Madame d', *Memoirs of the Court of England in 1675*, ed. George Gilbert (London, 1913)
Bagot, J., ed., *George Canning and his Friends*, ii (London, 1909)
Barr, Elaine, *George Wickes, 1698-1761* (London, 1980)
Barry, Alfred, *The Life and Works of Sir Charles Barry* (London, 1867)
Blakeborough, John Fairfax, *The Hunting and Sporting Reminiscences of H. W. Selby Lowndes* (London, 1926)
Boström, Antonia, 'A Rediscovered Florentine Bronze Group of the Rape of Proserpina at Cliveden', *Burlington Magazine*, cxxii (December 1990)
Boström, Antonia, 'Sculpture at Cliveden: A Connoisseur's Garden', *Apollo*, cxxii (August 1991)
Burghclere, Lady Winifred, *George Villiers, Second Duke of Buckingham* (London, 1903)
Burke, John Bernard, *The Romance of the Aristocracy* (London, 1855)
Burnet, Gilbert, *History of his Own Time*, i and ii (Oxford, 1724-34)
Butler, J. R. M., *Lord Lothian, 1882-1940* (London, 1960)
Campbell, Colen, *Vitruvius Britannicus*, ii (London, 1717)
Carr, Raymond, *English Fox Hunting: A History* (London, 1976)
Chapman, Hester W., *Great Villiers: A study of George Villiers, Second Duke of Buckingham* (London, 1949)
Churchill, Winston S., *Great Contemporaries* (London, 1937)
Christie, W. D., ed., 'Letters Addressed from London to Sir Joseph Williamson . . . 1673 and 1674', *Camden Society*, new series ii (1874)
Cockburn, Claud, *Crossing the Line* (London, 1958)
Cockett, Richard, *David Astor and the Observer* (London, 1991)
Collis, Maurice, *Nancy Astor* (London, 1960)
Colvin, Howard, *A Biographical Dictionary of British Architects, 1600-1840* (London, 1978)
Cornforth, John, 'Trentham, Staffordshire', I, II and III, *Country Life*, cxliii (25 January, 1 and 8 February 1968)
Cowles, Virginia, *The Astors* (New York, 1979)
Croker, J. W., ed., *Letters to and from Henrietta, Countess of Suffolk, and her Second Husband, the Hon George Berkeley, 1712-1767*, i (London, 1824)
Cummings, William, *Doctor Arne and 'Rule, Britannia'* (London, 1912)
Curties, Henry, *A Forgotten Prince of Wales* (London, 1912)
Cust, Lionel, *Records of the Cust Family*, series 3 (London, 1927)
Dalton, Charles, *George the First's Army, 1714-27*, i, (London, 1910)
Denning, Lord, *Lord Denning's Report* (London, September 1963)
Dibdin, Edward Rimbault, 'The Bi-centenary of Rule Britannia', *Music and Letters*, xxi (1940)
Disraeli, Benjamin, *Lothair* (London, 1870)
Dodington, George Bubb, *The Political Journals of George Bubb Dodington*, ed. John Carswell and L. A. Dralle (London, 1965)
Drake, Francis, *The History and Antiquities of the City of York* (London, 1736)
Dryden, John, *The Miscellaneous Works of John Dryden*, i (London, 1760)
Egmont, Earl of, *Diary of the First Earl of Egmont*, i, ii and iii (London, 1920-3)
Elliott, Brent, 'John Fleming Trendsetter', *The Garden* (February 1992)
Ervine, St John, *Bernard Shaw: His Life, Work and Friends* (London, 1956)
Evelyn, John, *The Diary of John Evelyn*, ed. E. S. De Beer, iv (London, 1955)
Fairfax, Brian, *Memoirs of the Life of George Villiers, Duke of Buckingham*, ed. Edward Arber (London, 1869)
Farington, Joseph, *The Farington Diaries*, ed. James Greig, i-vi (2nd edn London, 1922-7)
Fiske, Roger, 'A Cliveden Setting', *Music and Letters*, xlvii (1966)
Fleming, John, 'Spring and Winter Flower Gardening', *Journal of Horticulture* (1864)
Fulford, Roger, ed., *Your Dear Letter* (London, 1971)
'George Villiers, Second Duke of Buckingham', *Quarterly Review*, 187 (January 1898)
Gibbon, Edward, *My Journal*, ed. D. M. Low (London, 1929)
Gibbs, Vicary, and others, *The Complete Peerage* (London, 1910-40)
Gladstone, W. E., *The Gladstone Diaries*, ed. H. C. G. Matthew, iii-vi (London, 1974-8)
Godfrey, W. H., 'George Devey, 1820-1886: A Biographical Essay', *Journal of the Royal Institute of British Architects* (28 July 1906)
Gollin, Alfred, *'The Observer' and J. L. Garvin, 1908-1914* (Oxford, 1960)
Gower, Lord Ronald Sutherland, *My Reminiscences*, i (3rd edn London, 1884)
Gower, Lord Ronald Sutherland, *Old Diaries, 1881-1901* (London, 1902)
Green, David, *Gardener to Queen Anne: Henry Wise, 1653-1738, and The Formal Garden* (Oxford, 1956)
Green, Mary, ed., *Calendar of the Proceedings of the Committee for Compounding and Cases, 1647-June 1650* (London, 1891)
Grenfell, Joyce, *Darling Ma* (London, 1988)
Grenfell, Joyce, *In Pleasant Places* (London, 1979)
Greville, Charles, *The Greville Memoirs*, iii, ed. Henry Reeve (4th edn London, 1875)
Grey, Anchitell, *Debates of the House of Commons, 1667-1694*, ii (London, 1769)
Grigg, John, *Nancy Astor: Portrait of a Pioneer* (London, 1980)
Gronow, R. H., *The Reminiscences and Recollections of Captain Gronow, 1810-1860* (repr. London, 1985)
Hakewill, James, *The History of Windsor and its Neighbourhood* (London, 1813)
Hamilton, Anthony, *Memoirs of Count Grammont*, ed. Alan Fea (London, 1906)
Harrison, Rosina, *Rose: My Life in Service* (London, 1975)
Harrison, Rosina, *Gentleman's Gentleman: My Friends in Service* (London, 1976)
Haslam, Richard, 'Cliveden, Buckinghamshire', *Country Life*, clxxix (10 April 1986)
Herbage, Julian, *Arne: His Character and Environment* (London, 1960)
Hervey, Lord, *Lord Hervey's Memoirs*, ed. R. Sedgewick (London, 1952)
Hervieu, Auguste, *Revival of Pictorial Decoration in England* (London, 1856)
History and Proceedings of the House of Lords from

1660 to the Present Time, i (London, 1742)

Hodgkinson, Terence, 'Companions of Diana at Cliveden', *National Trust Studies* (London, 1979)

Hudson, Timothy, 'A Venetian Architect in England: Giacomo Leoni', *Country Life*, clvii (3 April 1975)

Hunting, Penelope, *The Life and Work of Henry Clutton, 1819-93*, PhD dissertation (London, 1979)

Hussey, Christopher, 'Cliveden, Bucks', I and II, *Country Life*, lxx (11 and 18 July 1931)

Huxley, Gervas, *Victorian Duke: The Life of Hugh Lupus Grosvenor* (London, 1967)

Irving Clive, *Scandal 63* (London, 1963)

Ivanov, Yevgeny, *The Naked Spy* (London, 1992)

Jackson-Stops, Gervase, *An English Arcadia* (London, 1992)

Jackson-Stops, Gervase, 'Cliveden, Buckinghamshire', I and II, *Country Life,* clxi (24 February and 3 March 1977)

Jackson-Stops, Gervase, *Cliveden*, National Trust guide (London, 1990, rev. Jonathan Marsden, 1994)

Jackson-Stops, Gervase, 'The Cliveden Album', I and II, *Architectural History*, xix (1976) and xx (1977)

Jackson-Stops, Gervase, 'Formal Garden Designs for Cliveden: The Work of Claude Desgots and Others for the 1st Earl of Orkney', *National Trust Year Book* (London, 1977)

James, Henry, *William Wetmore Story and his Friends* (Edinburgh and London, 1903)

Johnson, Samuel, and Chalmers, Alexander, eds, *The Works of the English Poets*, xi (London, 1810)

Jones, Thomas, *Whitehall Diary*, ed. Keith Middlemas (Oxford, 1969)

Jones, Stephen, *Frederick Prince of Wales and his Circle*, exh. cat. Gainsborough's House, Suffolk (June - July 1981)

Kavaler, Lucy, *The Astors: A Family Chronicle* (London, 1966)

Keeler, Christine, *Scandal* (London, 1989)

Kennedy, Ludovic, *The Trial of Stephen Ward* (London, 1964)

Knightley, Phillip, and Kennedy, Caroline, *An Affair of State* (London, 1987)

Knightley, Phillip, and Kennedy, Caroline, 'Who Saved the Royal Face?', *Illustrated London News*, 275 (July 1987)

Knightley, Phillip, and Simpson, Colin, *The Secret Lives of Lawrence of Arabia* (London, 1969)

Langhorne, Elizabeth, *Nancy Astor and her Friends* (New York, 1974)

Leconfield, Lady, and Gore, John, eds, *Three Howard Sisters* (London, 1955)

Leland, John, *The Itinerary of John Leland, the Antiquary*, ed. T. Hearne, ii (3rd edn Oxford, 1769)

Lewis, S., *A Topographical Dictionary of England*, iv (1831)

Lipscomb, George, *History and Antiquities of the County of Buckinghamshire*, ii and iii (London, 1847)

Lomax, E., and Gunyon, T. *Nicholson's Dictionary of the Science and Practice of Architecture*, i and ii (London and New York, 1857)

Macky, John, *A Journey through England*, i (5th edn London, 1732)

Markham, Clements R., *A Life of the Great Lord Fairfax* (London, 1870)

Markham, Sarah, *John Loveday of Caversham, 1711-1789* (Wilton, Wilts, 1984)

Marples, Morris, *Poor Fred and the Butcher* (London, 1870)

Martin, Theodore, *The Life of His Royal Highness the Prince Consort*, ii (3rd edn London, 1876)

Masters, Anthony, *Nancy Astor* (London, 1981)

Melton, Frank, 'Absentee Land Management in Seventeenth Century England', *Agricultural History* (1978)

Millar, Oliver, 'Notes on the Royal Collection', I, *Burlington Magazine*, cii (September 1961)

Millar, Oliver, *Tudor, Stuart and Early Georgian Pictures in the collection of H. M. The Queen* (London, 1963)

Morley, John, *The Life of William Ewart Gladstone*, ii, (New York, 1903)

Munnings, Alfred, *The Finish* (London, 1951)

Munnings, Alfred, *Pictures of Horses and English Life* (London, 1927)

Munnings, Alfred, *The Second Burst* (London, 1951)

Nimocks, Walter, *Milner's Young Men* (London, 1970)

O'Brien, Donough, *History of the O'Briens* (London, 1949)

Oldfield, Susan H., *Some Records of the Later Life of Harriet, Countess Granville* (London, 1901)

Page, William, ed., *The Victoria History of the Counties of England: A History of Buckinghamshire* iii (repr. London, 1969)

Pakula, Hannah, *The Last Romantic: a Biography of Queen Marie of Roumania* (London, 1985)

Patch, Blanche, *Thirty Years with G. B. S.* (London, 1951)

Pearson, Hesketh, *Bernard Shaw: His Life and Personality* (London, 1942)

Pepys, Samuel, *The Diary of Samuel Pepys*, ix, ed. Latham and Matthews (London, 1976)

Pevsner, Nikolaus, *The Buildings of England: Buckinghamshire* (London, 1960)

Pope, Alexander, *The Works of Alexander Pope*, iii, (London, 1881)

Powys, Caroline, *Passages from the Diaries of Mrs Philip Lybbe Powys* , cd. E. J. Climenson (London, 1899)

Pritchard, Allan, 'A Defence of his Private Life by the Second Duke of Buckingham', *Huntington Library Quarterly* (1981)

Quin, Anthony, *John Loughborough Pearson* (New Haven and London, 1979)

Reresby, John, *Memoirs of Sir John Reresby*, ed. Andrew Browning (Glasgow, 1936)

Richards, Eric, *The Leviathan of Wealth: The Sutherland Fortune in the Industrial Revolution* (London and Toronto, 1973)

Robert, C., 'A Collection of Roman Sarcophagi at Cliveden', *Journal of Hellenic Studies*, xx (1900)

Rorschach, Kimerly, *Frederick Prince of Wales as a Patron of the Visual Arts*, PhD dissertation (Yale, 1985)

Royal Commission on Historical Manuscripts, Ninth Report, Part 2, Appendix and Index (London, 1884)

Scott, Alexander, 'Arne's "Alfred"', *Music and Letters*, iv (October 1974)

Sinclair, David, *Dynasty* (London, 1983)

Stanhope, Philip Dormer, 4th Earl of Chesterfield, *Letters of the Earl of Chesterfield to his Son*, iv, ed. with intro. by B. Dobree (London, 1932)

Summers, Anthony, and Dorril, Stephen, *Honeytrap: The Secret Worlds of Stephen Ward* (London, 1987)

Swift, Jonathan, *The Works of Jonathan Swift*, iii, x, xv and ixx (Edinburgh, 1814)

Sykes, Christopher, *Nancy: The Life of Lady Astor* (London, 1972)

Taylor, Carole, 'Handel and Frederick, Prince of Wales', *Musical Times* cxxv (1984)

Thorne, R. G. , ed., *The History of Parliament: The House of Commons, 1790-1820* (London, 1986)

Thurlow, David, *The Hate Factor* (London, 1992)

Tyack, Geoffrey, *Cliveden and the Astor Household Between the Wars* (High Wycombe, 1982)

Tyack, Geoffrey, 'Service on the Cliveden Estate Between the Wars', *Journal of the Oral History Society*, v, no. 1 (Spring 1977)

Vertue, George, 'Vertue Note Books', I, *Walpole Society*, xviii (1930)

Villiers, George, 2nd Duke of Buckingham, *The Rehearsal*, ed. Edward Arber (repr. London, 1868)

Villiers, George, *The Works of His Grace George Villiers Late Duke of Buckingham*, 2 vols (London, 1715)

Walker, David, 'William Burn: The Country House in Transition' *Seven Victorian Architects*, ed. Jane Fawcett (London, 1976)

Walters, John, *The Royal Griffen* (London, 1972)

Ward-Jackson, Philip, 'A.-E. Carrier-Belleuse, J.-J. Feuchère and the Sutherlands', *Burlington Magazine*, 127 (March 1985)

Weaver, Lawrence, 'Cliveden, Bucks', I and II, *Country Life*, xxxii (7 and 14 December 1912)

Whiffen, Marcus, *Thomas Archer* (London, 1950)

Wilson, Derek, 'A Great Might-have-been', *The House Magazine* (8 March 1993)

Wilson, Derek, *The Astors, 1763-1992: Landscape with Millionaires* (London, 1993)

Wilson, John, *A Rake and his Times: George Villiers, 2nd Duke of Buckingham* (London, 1954)

Winn, James Anderson, *John Dryden and his World* (New Haven and London, 1987)

INDEX

PICTURE CREDITS

Illustrations appear by kind permission of the following: Viscount Astor 42 top, 44, 45 right, 47 bottom, 76 bottom, 79, 87, 103 left, 111, 113, 125 top, 130, 142 top, 143, 144, 152-3, 154, 156 top, 163 right, 177; Viscount Astor (photo. National Trust Picture Library) 43, 50-51, 73, 74-5, 94, 97, 99, 100; Viscount Astor, on loan to the National Trust (photo. Cliveden Hotel) 129; Bronwen, Viscountess Astor 189; British Architectural Library, R.I.B.A. 83; Lord Bruntisfield 81, 84 right; Buckinghamshire Record Office 107, 146, 148; Castle Howard collection 95, 96; Christie's Images 69; Cliveden Hotel viii, 22, 37, 40, 41, 58, 71 left, 84 left, 88-9, 97 bottom right, 103 right, 119, 127, 140, 164, 182, 187 right, 206, 208, 209, 210, 212; Conway Library, Courtauld Institute of Art 98 bottom; James Crathorne title page, 12, 21 32-3, 38, 39, 42 bottom, 45 left, 46, 47 top, 49, 54 left, 71 right, 72,76 top, 101, 104, 112 bottom, 113, 121, 124, 135, 137, 138, 139, 147, 183, 185, 191, 204, 205, 224; Duchy of Cornwall Archives 58 top, 60, 64, 66; E.T. Archive 23; Mary Evans Picture Library 66; Lark Gilmer 48, 97 top, 114-15, 133, 134, 149, 151, 161, 181 left, 192-3, 200-1, 207; G.L.C. Record Office 30; Grosvenor Estate, by kind permission of His Grace The Duke of Westminster, D.L 117, 125 bottom, 126; Honolulu Academy of Arts (gift of Judge John E. Parkes, 1987) 36; Hulton Deutsch Collection 107 right, 187 left; *London Evening Standard*, Solo Syndication 173; Lucinda Lambton 203; Mansell Collection 13, 27, 106; National Portrait Gallery, London 11, 17, 31, 59 bottom; 105, 109 bottom, 157, 181 right; National Trust at Cliveden (photo. Cliveden Hotel) 53, 54 right, 55, 57, 91, 141, 171; National Trust, Thames and Chilterns Region 103 left, 108, 109 top, 110, 112 top, 122, 123, 142 bottom; Ormond Family, 136; Private Collections 63, 78 top, 158-9, 168; Royal Collection, by kind permission of Her Majesty The Queen 61; Eddie Ryle-Hodges 211; Stanford University Centre in Oxford 195, 196, 197, 198; Countess of Sutherland (photo. Photographic Records Ltd) 93; Victoria Art Gallery, Bath City Council 77; University of Reading 155, 156 bottom, Yale Center for British Art, Paul Mellon Collection 15; Westminster City Archives 120.

Travertine fountain forming one end of the Borghese Balustrade on the Parterre.